Voices of Worcester Women

160 Years after the First National Woman's Rights Convention

Charlene L. Martin
and
Maureen Ryan Doyle

Copyright © 2011 by Charlene L. Martin and Maureen Ryan Doyle
All rights reserved.

No part of this book may be reproduced, stored in a retrieval system, or transmitted in any form without the prior written permission of the authors.

The interviewees' statements do not necessarily reflect the views of the authors. Quotes are from interviews conducted with permission to reproduce or publish and have been edited only for the purpose of clarity.

ISBN-13: 978-1466361539
ISBN-10: 1466361530

Cover Design by Breeana Goodrow

Photographs Provided by Interviewees

Printed in the United States of America

Dedication

To my mother, Mary Sweeney Ryan, for showing me that every woman is of value. And to my aunt, Edna Mae Sweeney, for teaching me that nothing is more fascinating than history.

> Maureen Ryan Doyle

In memory of my mother, Mary Arcieri Longhi, who taught me the importance of listening to people's stories.

> Charlene L. Martin

CONTENTS

	Acknowledgments	vii
	Foreword	1
1.	Worcester Women's Oral History Project	5
2.	Education	14
3.	Work	58
4.	Health	93
5.	Politics/Community Involvement	132
6.	Uniquely Worcester Remembrances	160
	Bibliography	187
	Index	189
	About the Authors	190

ACKNOWLEDGMENTS

We owe deep and abiding gratitude to Linda Rosenlund whose vision and perseverance created the Worcester Women's Oral History Project (WWOHP); to Melanie Demarais for our initial nomination to the Steering Committee of the Worcester Women's History Project (WWHP); to the Schlesinger Library on the History of Women in America at the Radcliffe Institute of Harvard University, the official repository of WWOHP transcripts and recordings, for financial support that helped to make this publication possible; to Dr. Lisa Krissoff Boehm, oral historian at Worcester State University for her ongoing support of WWOHP; to Dr. John McClymer, an extraordinary professor of History at Assumption College, who recommended that we pursue the publication of this work; to William Wallace, Executive Director of the Worcester Historical Museum for providing a home to WWHP; and to the members of WWHP and WWOHP who are dedicated to raising the awareness of Worcester's role in the women's rights movement.

WWOHP's success is due in large part to the many professors within the colleges of Worcester who agree to include oral history into their curricula and to their students who conduct and transcribe the interviews. Our thanks to each of them for the over 250 oral histories collected to date.

We thank all the women who agreed to have their life stories recorded by WWOHP. Perhaps history never expected to hear their voices, but we know that history is forever changed because of their honesty and candor.

Maureen would like to thank her husband, Frank, who is her greatest source of encouragement and support; Maryssa, Colin, and Dani Doyle who continually delight and embolden her; and the wonderful community of Worcester that continues to inspire and support women of all ages.

Charlene would like to thank her husband, Jim, for always listening to her stories.

FOREWORD

Interviewing people can change lives. It changed mine.

"I don't know why you want to talk to me. I don't know anything and I have little to share." After requesting an interview, I heard that response from women far too often. It's been my experience that those who consider themselves to be ordinary feel vulnerable and are mystified as to why anyone would have an interest in capturing their memories and experiences.

My grandmother felt that way. She was a seemingly ordinary woman, without prestige, education, or wealth. Her mother emigrated from Italy in the early 20th century, not knowing how to read or write. Both of them were happy in their spheres, taking care of their husbands and family; keeping a clean, happy home; and being a good neighbor.

Although she gladly shared many stories of the "good old days" during visits at her home, Gram didn't understand the historical value of sharing her experiences of living with immigrant parents, of the hardships endured during the Great Depression, of neighbors putting Gold Stars in their windows after losing sons in World War II, or of working as a seamstress a few hours a week to supplement the family's income.

I knew that ordinary women are often invisible to the historical record and, while serving as president of the Worcester Women's History Project (WWHP), I fully

1

embraced the idea of a local oral history project that would be inclusive of women from all walks of life. The steering committee ultimately decided that a community-based oral history project would enable the organization to achieve its goals of broadly including the contributions of women throughout Central Massachusetts.

Since its founding in 2005 the Worcester Women's *Oral* History Project (WWOHP) understood the value of documenting "ordinary" women, because they, too, are significant interpreters and participants in history and are often the glue that holds a community together.

As a past president of WWHP and the founding chair of the Worcester Women's Oral History Project (WWOHP), I have worked with many committed local women and men, who gave their time and talents to strengthen our community's historical record by documenting the contributions of local women.

WWOHP will be forever grateful to Lisa Krissoff Boehm who served as the professional consultant to the project. A nationally acclaimed oral historian and history professor at Worcester State University, Lisa was one of the first to respond to a call from WWHP to create a taskforce made up of representatives from local colleges to lay the groundwork for the project. Through Lisa's efforts and expertise, WWOHP was created following the highest professional standards in preserving source material and making it available to others.

Lisa was also helpful serving with a group of local professors to create a "higher education collaboration" that would involve students in conducting oral history interviews. This collaborative became a sustaining feature of WWOHP by generating scores of interviews each year and providing transcriptions of each.

A debt of gratitude is also owed to Erin Anderson who provided invaluable assistance in helping to map out the project. Then a graduate student in Community

Development and Planning at Clark University, Erin first became involved as a volunteer and later served as an extraordinary intern. In addition to the many hours she spent on the Project, including her assistance organizing workshops for community outreach, she met with me weekly for nearly a year at a local coffee shop to help sort out the many intricacies and myriad of issues while planning the ambitious project.

Without the expertise of Lisa and the assistance of Erin, WWOHP would not be where it is today – groundbreaking in its level of collaboration, community engagement, and scope. Still, in all of the planning, I had never envisioned the day when we would have collected more than 250 interviews and, in addition, WWOHP's collection of interviews would be accepted at the Schlesinger Library on the History of Women in America, located at the Radcliffe Institute of Harvard University.

As often happens in life, stories come full circle, intersecting along the way. In a wonderful stroke of synchronicity, just when new leadership was needed for WWOHP, Charlene Longhi Martin and Maureen Ryan Doyle joined the steering committee of the Worcester Women's History Project in 2007 and agreed to co-chair the Project the following year.

Charlene, Maureen, and I share a special bond through our Assumption College connection. We are alumnae, we have worked at the College, and it was fun to discover that Charlene had been employed as a work-study student for Maureen in the Public Relations Office in the 1970s, and I was a work-study student in the Continuing Education Office, working for Charlene in the 1980s.

Charlene and Maureen have fully embraced the Project and have found innovative ways to keep it moving forward. Their first goal was to organize the collection of interview tapes, transcripts, and supporting documentation to ensure the preservation and consistent format of the materials, increasing the possibility of the collection's acceptance by an esteemed repository, such as the Schlesinger Library.

Steadfast in their leadership, Charlene and Maureen's tireless efforts have enabled WWOHP to thrive as a living oral history. They chair a reinvigorated committee that offers community oral history workshops, conducts classroom tutorials, and hosts an annual public program featuring an oral historian that is open to the community.

By researching the oral history transcripts of women who were interviewed as part of WWOHP and compiling these excerpts into a book, Charlene and Maureen have given Central Massachusetts a wonderful gift. Together these stories underlie the importance of preserving memories as well as providing a glimpse into the voices of a community in vivid, plainly spoken terms.

WWOHP hopes to inspire you to ask someone for their story. Document it. Capture their experiences. Share it, not only because of the pleasure it will bring, but because of the tremendous resource it will be to your family and to your community.

One of the greatest gifts of my life has been when interviewees, especially reluctant women who had to be persuaded to share their story, thank me profusely after the interview. Recently an elderly woman, who was terminally ill, looked at me when the recording device was turned off and said, "Oh, that was a wonderful trip ... I had forgotten how special my life has been ..."

Linda Burlingame Rosenlund
Founding Chair, Worcester
Women's Oral History Project
August 11, 2011

CHAPTER ONE

WORCESTER WOMEN'S ORAL HISTORY PROJECT

"Now let us see what all this balderdash, clap-trap, rant, cant, fanaticism, and blasphemy means….."

> James Gordon Bennett editorial, *New York Herald*, October 28, 1850

You are invited to join us as we delve into the complexities and intricacies of the lives of some fascinating women. The Worcester Women's Oral History Project (WWOHP) is the newest initiative of the Worcester Women's History Project (WWHP). Our purpose is to build community by sharing experiences through women's stories. We are devoted to recording, collecting, and sharing the personal and historical memories of women throughout the Worcester and Central Massachusetts community. The Project focuses on women of all ages, ethnicities, and socio-economic backgrounds. We believe it is not just the well known and privileged who have stories to tell. The goals, dreams, challenges, and successes of everyday women bring history alive, allowing you, the reader, a richer and fuller vision of the past.

The Worcester Women's History Project (WWHP) was established in 1994 by Lisa Connelly Cook and a small group of women and men to increase awareness of the prominent role Worcester, Massachusetts played in the abolition and suffrage movements in the 19th century, and in particular to highlight the importance of the First National Woman's Rights Convention that was held in Worcester in 1850.

Most historians point to the 1848 regional meeting at Seneca Falls as the origin of the women's rights movement. While certainly of importance, it was not national in scope. Three hundred people attended from within a five-mile radius. Referring to the meeting, Elizabeth Cady Stanton stated, "It will start women thinking and men too; and when men and women think about a new question, the first step in progress is taken."

It is the Worcester 1850 Convention that was the first organized and nationwide call to action. Attendance was estimated at 1,000 people, including delegates from many of the states and some European countries. There was great positive reaction to the published proceedings, both in the U.S. and in Europe. Standing committees were formed, in addition to a Central Committee, to address the issues raised on education, industrial avocations, civil and political functions, social relations, and publication.

In fact, the Worcester Convention was commemorated 20 years later at the 1870 Convention at Apollo Hall in New York City, and advertised as "The Twentieth Anniversary of the Inauguration of the Woman Suffrage Movement" in this country. Elizabeth Cady Stanton issued the call to the 1870 meeting. She also proposed that the presiding officer of the 1850 meeting in Worcester,

Paulina Wright Davis, preside over the 1870 convention in New York. The importance and significance of the 1850 First National Woman's Rights Convention in Worcester were sealed.

It is clear that the first wave of women's rights activists recognized and celebrated the fact that their national movement had its beginnings in Worcester in 1850. However, through the years, historians and students of history have lost sight of this. It is the mission of the Worcester Women's History Project to bring to the forefront the important role Worcester played in the struggle for women's rights. For it was at Brinley Hall on Main Street that it truly all began.

To better understand the significance of the First National Convention, it is important to consider the culture of 1850 and of Worcester, Massachusetts itself. Mid-nineteenth century America was a time of hope, invention, reform, and turbulence. In that year a patent was issued for the first dishwasher. Nathaniel Hawthorne completed *The Scarlet Letter,* and the book was being criticized by a prominent minister who described it as a "brokerage of lust." California was admitted to the union as a free state, and The Fugitive Slave Act became law, requiring the return of slaves living in free states to their previous masters. The Abolitionist Movement was gaining momentum with each passing year, and the Underground Railroad was becoming more active.

Worcester was no stranger to this innovation and reform. It was teeming with entrepreneurs eager to make their fortunes in this newly industrialized age. More patents for new inventions were issued to Worcester County inhabitants than to those of any other in the 19th century, clearly ensuring Worcester's place on the forefront of change. Worcester was also a hotbed of political and religious fervor, as Abolitionists and those embracing the

Temperance Movement spoke regularly from Worcester podiums.

Yet it was still a time when many women had little voice. Surely, suffrage was but a distant dream, and those who worked on its behalf were often derided. While unthinkable by today's standards, many considered it indecent for women to speak in public forums addressing audiences comprised of both women and men. The moral character of the women who dared to proceed in these endeavors was often called into question. A woman's domain was considered to be hearth and home. Other pursuits were often considered unnatural for the fairer sex. In marriage in many states, it was the husband who owned the property, and at the altar it was the wife who promised to obey. What courage and conviction it took for those women who banded together and organized this First National Convention.

It also took hope, and drive, and fortitude. The climate of possibility and change was real in mid-19th century Worcester. The fact that over 1,000 individuals attended that First National Woman's Rights Convention in October of 1850 at Brinley Hall confirms that. The resolutions passed during the two-day Convention focused on increasing opportunities for women at all educational levels and in all professions; a co-equal share in the formation and administration of law; and the formation of a Central Committee, authorized to call other Conventions. As Abby H. Price, a Hopedale, Massachusetts activist in social reform movements, stated in her address, "Our daughters should fit themselves equally with our sons, for any post of usefulness and profit that they may choose."

The significance of the Convention was far reaching. The final resolution called for "equality before the law without distinction of sex or color." This statement that clearly urged equality for black women offended many. Despite controversy, outrage by critics, and belittlement by opponents, the significance of the Convention was far reaching and the organized movement for women's rights began its long struggle.

In October of 2000, the Worcester Women's History Project held a national three-day conference, *Women 2000*, to commemorate the 150th anniversary of the First National Woman's Rights Convention. The Conference was a mobilizing effort to continue the discussions that began in 1850. It also provided a platform to discuss the present status of women and to delve into the challenges of the future. Thirty workshops were presented including *A Political History of Women's Mental Health; Gender Justice: Women's Rights ARE Human Rights; Preserving Women's History: Seneca Falls, Worcester, and Beyond;* and *Women's Health Perspective: Where We Have Been and Where We Are Going.* In addition, a play dramatizing the first Convention was performed. *Angels and Infidels* was written by nationally recognized playwright Louisa Burns Bisogno and it was performed by a professional cast.

After the founders of the Worcester Women's History Project succeeded in their original goal to commemorate the 150th anniversary of the 1850 National Woman's Rights Convention with *Women 2000*, they decided to continue to work toward raising awareness of the Convention and of Worcester's role in the history of women's rights. Another significant achievement occurred when WWHP presented the Trustees of the Worcester County Mechanics Association with a gift of four portraits of distinguished 19th century women, all with deep ties to the Worcester area. Those portraits are of Clara Barton, founder of the American Red Cross; Dorothea Lynde Dix, a pioneer in the field of mental health who changed the treatment of the mentally ill in Massachusetts and then the nation; Abby Kelley Foster, the outspoken proponent of abolition and women's rights; and Lucy Stone, women's rights advocate and reformer. These portraits now hang in the Great Hall at

Mechanics Hall in Worcester. Prior to this, only portraits of notable men graced the walls of the Great Hall.

WWHP continues to promote the research and dissemination of historically significant information. It offers a dramatic one-woman play, *Yours for Humanity—Abby*, about Abby Kelley Foster, the leading 19th century human rights advocate who spent more than 20 years as a national lecturer for the American Anti-Slavery Society. At a time when the culture expected women to be quiet and obedient, Abby Kelley Foster instead worked steadfastly to end race and gender inequality. WWHP has also published the *Worcester Women's Heritage Trail: Worcester in the Struggle for Equality in the Mid-Nineteenth Century*. This booklet provides information about Worcester's early reformers and the places where they gathered. In 2000, WWHP designed, installed, and dedicated a plaque for Tuckerman Hall, in recognition of the former site of the Worcester Women's Club, and its architect, Josephine Wright Chapman. In addition, WWHP has developed history curricula for elementary and secondary schools, displayed exhibits at the Worcester Public Library during the month of March in celebration of Women's History Month, and presents public programming featuring women authors.

The mission of WWHP is ongoing. It seeks to raise awareness of the rich history of women in the Worcester area; create national recognition of Worcester's role in the history of the women's rights movement; and advance the ideal put forth in the 1850 convention that there should be "equality before the law, without distinction of sex or color," or ethnicity. The Worcester Women's Oral History Project (WWOHP) is an extension of the Worcester Women's History Project as it builds upon the core value that emphasizes "the discovery of connections between past and present, for the benefit of the future" and assists in achieving WWHP's goal to "facilitate the incorporation of women's contributions within the historical record." The Oral History

Project's focus is on women who are making history today as it aims to record, collect, and share the personal and historical memories of women throughout the Central Massachusetts community.

In its desire to record and preserve the stories of Worcester women of all backgrounds and generations, WWOHP seeks to build community by sharing experiences through the collection of women's stories. In this way, it supports the mission of WWHP to not only celebrate the past achievements of Worcester women, but to also preserve the accomplishments of the present generation.

Oral histories provide a richer understanding of people's everyday lives, goals, dreams, challenges, and successes. WWOHP through its work and this book hopes to share, with the readers of today and the historians of tomorrow, the stories and experiences of today's Worcester women and the challenges they face 160 years after the 1850 Convention.

WWOHP was launched in October 2005 as a major initiative of the Worcester Women's History Project. In the seven months following, a focus group of local college and university professors and professional oral historian Dr. Lisa Krissoff Boehm, met monthly to develop the Project. It was led by Linda Rosenlund and a subcommittee and by the end of 2006 a permanent committee was created. It was established that all interviews would be conducted in accordance with the guidelines of the Oral History Association. Informed consent and deeds of gift are obtained from all interviewees allowing their words to be made available to researchers worldwide.

One of the key elements of WWOHP's success was the creation of the Higher Education Collaborative. The Higher Education Collaborative entails working with local professors to involve college and university students in the collection and transcription of oral histories of Worcester women as a part of their coursework. Students have the opportunity to learn actively through hands-on experience with oral history and share their work with the Worcester community through public forums, in print, and online. This effort promotes innovative cross-institutional collaboration and engages students in the community in a respectful and meaningful way. Not only does the Project receive much-needed assistance from student volunteers, but students benefit by learning about the value of oral history preservation and about Worcester women and history.

There are other unique aspects of WWOHP that set it apart from other oral history projects including the fact that it is an all-volunteer effort. The committee members, students, and faculty all volunteer their time for the united effort of gathering the stories of Worcester women. The Project is also privileged to have many transcripts on the lives of Deaf women due to the involvement of students and faculty of the College of the Holy Cross Deaf Studies Program.

WWOHP is also innovative in its level of community engagement. It regularly provides community workshops on oral history (including one geared specifically toward the Hispanic community), as well as events featuring noted oral historians and college students' presentations on their interviewees. These workshops and events are held at local colleges, Worcester Public Library, and Worcester Historical Museum.

Almost 250 interviews have been collected, transcribed, and preserved at the time of publication and many full-text transcripts are available to the public on the Project's website. The Project is honored to have the Schlesinger Library as the repository for its oral histories. The Schlesinger Library on the History of Women in America is on the campus of Radcliffe Institute at Harvard University in Cambridge, MA and maintains collections relating to a wide range of American women's activities. It provides rich material for researchers and historians from around the world.

The oral histories collected by WWOHP focus on the four themes that characterize the spirit of the 1850 National Woman's Rights Convention held in Worcester: Work, Education, Health, and Politics/Community Involvement. These are some of the fundamental issues discussed and argued at the Convention and they also correlate with the committees established at the end of the Convention that marked the beginning of the first organized plan of action to continue the work of women's rights. This book is divided into these four themes plus a fifth theme: Uniquely Worcester Remembrances.

Our intent here is not to replicate complete and unedited transcripts of oral histories, but rather to provide a window into the life and times of some of the women chronicled by WWOHP. Our aim is to condense stories without altering the facts, tone, or meaning of the original transcripts. Therefore, there may be slight variations between the audiotapes and the stories that are printed here.

We owe deep gratitude to those women and men who fought the comfortable conformity of their age, and envisioned a new and brighter world of equality, opportunity, and respect. We honor them today, 160 years after the First National Woman's Rights Convention, by presenting the stories of today's women of Worcester. They are women from ages 18 to 103 and they represent various ethnic, socioeconomic, and religious backgrounds. These are their hopes, these are their memories, these are their lives.

We are delighted that you will take this journey with us. Keep in mind as we explore these stories that we can learn from each other. You may ask yourself how the experiences of these women are like your own. Or in what ways their challenges are different from what you have encountered. How far have we come? And how far do we still need to travel?

CHAPTER TWO

EDUCATION

"Under a true system of education—a system in which education will not be distinguished by gender—man and woman will find their respective spheres in life; and that too, by the free direction of their own inclinations."

> From L.A. Hine, Cincinnati, October 15, 1850
> Letter read on October 23, 1850 – morning session
> of the First National Woman's Rights Convention

In a review of the history of education in the United States, we learn that women had a long struggle to gain access to education—especially higher education. During Colonial times, the culture did not encourage independent thinking in women, despite the fact that wives often shared the difficult task of forging a new life in a new country alongside their husbands. After the American Revolution, women such as Abigail Adams and Mercy Warren advocated the need for the education of women. While the status of women was largely ignored by the founding fathers in the efforts to create a new republic, there were some men who believed that the education of women was essential to the nation because of their roles as mothers. Although women were not citizens, they were expected to educate their sons to be good citizens. This ideal of "Republican motherhood" became the first factor in swaying public opinion in support of education for women. Other factors included the growing need for teachers and the need for educated women to provide financial support to their families or themselves if not married.

In 1873, 23 years after the First National Woman's Rights Convention, Dr. Edward H. Clarke of Harvard Medical School and a member of the Massachusetts Medical Society, published his theories on women and education. Despite critics' claims of faulty methodology and data refuting his findings, Clarke's theory that women would endanger their physical bodies (and perhaps their possibilities of motherhood) if they spent too much time studying was widely circulated and believed. He stated, "She was unable to make a good brain, that could stand the wear and tear of life, and a good reproductive system that should serve the race, at the same time that she was continuously spending her force in intellectual labor." (Clarke 103) During a time when women were struggling to be accepted into the world of education, work, and politics, opponents were countering with arguments such as Dr. Clarke's.

While colleges eventually began to accept female students, the collegiate experience was different for the first female students than for male students. When women began attending coeducational colleges and universities, they were "outsiders" outnumbered by men and also restricted from much social interaction with them. Women lived, ate, exercised, and socialized almost exclusively with other women. Colleges had male traditions, male benefactors, and mostly male faculty, but these women pioneers persevered because of their strong desire for higher education.

Even in 1978, the President of Smith College, Jill Ker Conway, stated that despite federal laws such as Title IX and the Women's Educational Equity Act, it would be "a long time before the informal social environment in America's male-dominated colleges and universities will serve women students as well as men." (Conway 9) She explained that although women are provided access to the same classrooms, libraries, and facilities, they do not necessarily have the same experiences. She was not alone in perceiving that higher education was not necessarily a welcoming place for female students. A paper presented to the American Council on Education reported that the 1971 Newman Task Force "found that discrimination against women, in contrast to that against minorities, is still overt and socially acceptable within the academic community." (Cross 45)

American women first began to outnumber men in undergraduate higher education enrollment in the 1980s and in advanced degrees in 2010. One hundred and sixty years after the First National Woman's Rights Convention, we are interested in how women in Worcester have experienced education. This chapter includes their stories about access to schools and higher education as well as their life experiences and motivations. Some share their memories of elementary and high school years and others tell us what it was like for them during college or graduate school. Several relate the experience of being educators—a few as the first female professors in formerly all-male colleges. Whether attaining their education through traditional or non-traditional avenues, each communicates the meaning of education in her life.

> And why should girls be learn'd or wise?
> Books only serve to spoil their eyes.
> The studious eye but faintly twinkles
> And reading paves the way to wrinkles.
> John Trumbull, 1770s

Nora Antoun Hakim
Age 86
Interviewed on March 5, 2007 by Elizabeth Boosahda

We all have special teachers who influence us in our lives, and I had a very good English teacher, whose name was Miss Churchill, and somehow she kept on encouraging me. Well, at the time there was debate, and these contests in doing these readings in drama, both serious and comedic, and that sort of thing. And we went from one level to another; we were encouraged to participate in our own school, then on a regional level, and finally on a state level. And apparently, I did well enough to win in all those levels that I finally became eligible to go to the national contest, which happened to be in Hollywood, California. However, that happened at the same time that I was participating and speaking at my own graduation. This was senior year, and I had to choose between going to Hollywood [laughter] and participating in my class in graduation and I decided to stay home and participate in that.

My recollection was that my parents never had to urge me to do well in school or whatever, but it was just understood that I was expected to do as well as I could and, apparently, I didn't realize this until years later, but you know I excelled in certain areas and I was encouraged in those areas. So at any rate, at school—well, first they encouraged me to think about going to Yale Drama School, and the superintendent was good enough to spend a day taking me there to visit, but we found out when we arrived that the Drama School at Yale was a graduate school. So now, the closest school that gave me training in speech and drama was in Pittsburgh, Pennsylvania, and that was called Carnegie Tech [Carnegie Institute of Technology] at the time and is now called Carnegie Mellon [University]. Well, at any rate, that's how it happened and my parents agreed that I could go there and try out to see if I was eligible to enter that school. Well, I passed the test, and that's when I started my speech and drama training at Carnegie Tech. But I had told them there that I was interested in teaching and they suggested that I transfer to New York University in Manhattan because there was more training there along those lines. That's how I happened to now go to Manhattan which was a wonderful place to be in during that era. And you know the city itself was an education, but at any rate, I had my training there in speech and drama. And it was in my senior year that Pearl Harbor came on the scene and that, of course, led our entry into World War II.

So at the end of my senior year, a recruiter came to New York University and told us about these relocation centers ......on the west coast of our country, and there were, I think, ten of them at the time. My recollection is there was a General DeWitt who encouraged that we have these relocation centers for all the Japanese who lived on the West Coast. This hadn't even appeared in the papers in the East. I wasn't aware of them and I was very curious about how anything like that could happen in our country. So, I agreed to go out and teach in one of the relocation centers. They sent me to Arizona, to the largest of the relocation centers. There were about 20,000 Japanese there, and my assignment was to teach the Nisei (pronounced nee-say)—in other words, the young people who were born in this country. Their parents were not allowed to become citizens. So, I became a teacher of the Nisei there.

In my college years there were both men and women at Carnegie Tech and also at NYU, however, toward the end .... we had only one man left in class because people were recruited into the war. So it was very strange as all of a sudden you see most of the men were gone. Now this, of course, was during the war. And in those days there was rationing and we were all very patriotic, and we all wanted to be involved in some way. So in a sense, you see, my going to teach—because this was as a result of the war that the Japanese were put in those internment camps—well I felt, you know, this was helping out in one of the ways that we could.

They only had 48 hours' notice and they had to leave their homes, their businesses, their farms, everything. And the barracks that they had to live in—and we lived in—had to be put up in 48 hours. So we all lived in these barracks, and the teachers had just a very small room with the absolute necessities there, but the Japanese, for the Japanese, each barrack was divided into four, and they lived in one room, which was about 24 by 24 feet square, and a whole family lived in that one room.

And everything was communal....the mess halls were communal, their laundry was communal, and all the other facilities..... And we were really on the largest Indian reservation in our country—it was the Navajo Reservation—and we were on the desert on a corner of that reservation. It was so [desolate] there wasn't even any cactus there [laughter]. You see we had nothing there, it was like a blank canvas, and we didn't even have any books to teach with. So we had to be extremely creative to begin with. We helped finish building the school when we arrived there and it was sometime in the summer and I think the temperature was up to about 110.

So it was very pleasant teaching them......These young people would file in, all of them looking the same to me in the beginning. All of them, you know, looking Japanese with their slanted eyes, their skin color the same and so on, and I thought, "How am I going to be able to tell them apart?" Well, pretty soon, you saw that color didn't matter, that everybody was an individual no matter what their race or color was, and pretty soon, I just saw them all as individuals. And that has stayed with me all my life—that color doesn't matter, we are all God's children [laughter].

Hannah Laipson
Age 83
Interviewed on November 14, 2008
by Andrea Gagnon
and Danielle Buttafuoco of
Assumption College

I went to Colby College in Waterville, Maine, and loved it there, and that was during the period of World War II. I majored in English at Colby and minored in History. I was always very interested in History and Politics and after I graduated from college, that was when the servicemen were returning from the service. My husband and I got married when he got out of the service and we went back to UMass [University of Massachusetts] Amherst so that he could finish his last year and a half. And I worked out there. The first semester I got a job, a clerical job, at Amherst College, working for the head of the Geology Department. And then the second semester, I had met the head of the English Department in Amherst at a social gathering and while talking I told him I was an English major and he called me one day. Could I pitch in and substitute for somebody who had left unexpectedly just before the semester started? So here I was, a brand-new graduate, and I'm teaching sophomore survey of English literature. But what was really funny about that experience was that several of my students were quite a bit older than I was. They were returning G.I.'s [Government Issue—used in reference to an enlisted person in the United States Armed Forces] from the service, and I still remember there was one fellow who used to sit in the back row who was a veteran. Every time his hand went up my heart sunk because he'd ask me these difficult questions and I was a new fledgling at a time. But I learned to cope with that and admit when I wasn't sure of the answer.

Teaching has been a part of my life in one way or another because even while my first child was one year old, I started teaching three times a week at Temple Emmanuel [in Worcester, MA], which was where we belonged. When my youngest, when my son was about 11—are you familiar with the writings of Betty Friedan? She was the feminist—she was the first great [modern] writer of feminism and she wrote a book that became immensely popular, and when I read it, I decided it was time for me to do something more. So that was when I enrolled at Assumption [College] for my Master's degree, and from that point on, I was a teacher.

When I say education has been a very important part of my life, teaching at a community college was a really special experience. I was at Assumption for four years, and the students were, I would say, 98 percent in those days were from parochial schools, and the classes reflected that quite a bit. I think it was the fourth year that I was teaching here, it was, or it might have been in 1970, those were the years, the late '60s and early '70s, when the most popular writers, the novelists, were the American-Jewish writers. There was Saul Bellow, Bernard Malamud, Philip Roth, and a whole score of others. So I introduced to the English Department, the possibility, what would they think of my giving a course in American-Jewish writers? And I had written my Master's thesis on that. So they said, "Sure, that sounds great, go ahead." Well, everybody in the department laughed—about 140 students signed up for the class! So instead of my teaching two sessions, I had to teach three sessions, and it was a wonderful experience and I still remember and I quote it sometimes—here is this class of Catholic students, and we're talking about all these American-Jewish writers who were emerging from their very different experiences and we were reading—Phillip Roth at that time was not my favorite writer but I felt I had to include him. One of his best-seller books at that time was *Goodbye Columbus*. And we were discussing that book and one of the students raised his hand, he was Italian, and he said to me, "What's so Jewish about Aunt Gladys? She sounds exactly like my aunt!" [Laughs]. So we had good interchange like that and it was very successful and worked out very well.

Then I went off to a community college [Quinsigamond Community College] which was a totally different experience. My students ranged from the age of 17 to 75. I could have all types of students in my classes, some of whom were so bright they could have been at any college in the country and some of whom had been working and felt there was more to life than just this and they were coming back to school for that, and some who didn't have a clue. So you dealt with all those different experiences and it was very wonderful. I really got a lot out of those 20 years, I must say. I met wonderful teachers there and the stress was on helping the students.

When I retired, I knew that I had to have some structure, but I still couldn't get away from education. And at that point the WISE [Worcester Institute for Senior Education at Assumption College] program was started and I was on the first Council. It was actually started by seven social workers who felt that in retirement they wanted to do something more stimulating than just going to out to lunch or playing cards. One of them had heard of a program through Elderhostel, which you may have heard of, and they contacted Elderhostel, and that was how WISE began. And also they worked through the Consortium of Colleges in Worcester. And the head of the consortium said to them, "You can't have a board with seven social workers. You have to get some other people involved in the first board so that you have more diversity." So that's when I was called by somebody, a dentist was brought in, somebody in another profession, some business people were, so for the next 13 years I taught an English course every year as a volunteer group leader and I served as curriculum chair and eventually became President of WISE for two years. But I enjoyed the education part all the time and go as a student. Every year I sign up for courses and my husband does too. So that's a wonderful way to keep your mind working, and not dwell on the fact that you're not quite as energetic as you may have been when you were 25.

I still serve on the board because when you're President of the organization, you're automatically on the board forever [laughs]. And I still serve on the curriculum committee where we decide on the courses and call people to lead the courses for us. We have people from all the colleges in the city. And we draw on Assumption very heavily of course because [of] our director, who is the liaison at Assumption—and so it's a wonderful experience, it really is. I finally—about a year ago—I said it's time for my second retirement so that's when I stopped teaching. But I'm still fully involved.

The members of WISE have all different types of educations but they are educated from the perspective of life experience. Many have graduate degrees; many are professionals, business owners, executives, all kinds of things. Some are people who just lived at home and raised their children…tremendous diversity. So often, somebody will say to me, knowing that I'm on the curriculum committee, "You know, this time, I didn't find anything that interested me." So I've coined a new reply to that, and that is, "Take something that doesn't interest you, you might be really surprised at what you'll find." For example, I took one course at UMass Medical [School]. I'm not scientifically inclined. I struggled with my science courses, I did okay, but I had to really work hard. I was always more on the humanities. I took this course, I thought "Gee, that might be interesting," which consisted of five research professors from UMass Medical. They were so skilled and so intelligent; I came out of each session just loving it. Now, it was completely out of my sphere, but it was an opening and I would encourage anybody else who felt the way I did to go do the same type of thing.

Dorian Ross (Pseudonym)
Age 80
Interviewed on October 23, 2007 by Claire Rheaume of Worcester State University

My mother's uncle was knighted as a physician in England. When [Queen] Elizabeth's grandfather had cancer of the throat, he was the one who was brought in… and so he was knighted. My grandmother, my mother's mother, was known as being a midwife and an herbalist… I guess what we would call a physician's assistant. Even though I didn't know them, they were kind of like heroes in my life. I wanted to be like them.

My mother came from Bermuda where my brother and sister were from too. From New York City, we moved to the country [upstate New York]. I had good teachers there. I was at the top of my class. There were 18 kids in the whole eight grades. One teacher, no electricity… the teacher had flashlights.

You know you aren't supposed to be on third shift when you're just 17, but I did. They didn't enforce them during the war years. Just like when I was in high school, I was 13 and you had to be 14 to get working papers. So since my mother was in the hospital, my teacher and principal signed the papers to say that I was 14… and I got working papers. I quit in the middle of my junior year to work and I didn't get half as much attention when I got back to school, because I had three jobs… one was part-time the other two were full.

I left teachers' college in the middle of my junior year and went to Washington D.C. They gave me money because I had none. I went to Howard University. I had to maintain a B average to keep my full scholarship. The faculty and others, whom I didn't even know, gave me their support.

I had arthritis, but I recovered from it. I graduated from graduate school in 1949. A dean found out that I had been working as a cashier at a supper club. I had a part-time job, and when he found out, he made me quit. Boys could work there, but not girls. Not at a supper club. He could take his wife there for dinner, but he made me quit.

I was very fortunate when I was in high school and said when I was a freshman in high school I wanted to be a doctor. One side said that I couldn't be a doctor because I was poor, and I didn't have a father. Others said, "Just look at you,"—whatever I was. In this country, if you're not white you're black, no matter whether you're Native American, or whatever. I just hate that. I wish that they just wouldn't throw so much hate around. After a while, your dream comes true, and you are what you want to be. I got a wonderful occupation. Learned more and more and more and more. Here I'm in the Intergenerational Urban Institute at Worcester State College. Additionally, I'm on the Massachusetts Senior Action Council. We are called a senior lobby. I volunteer at MedCity [Hospital].

Claire Quintal
Age 78
Interviewed on March 17, 2009 by Meredith Deacon
and Melanie Hentz of Assumption College

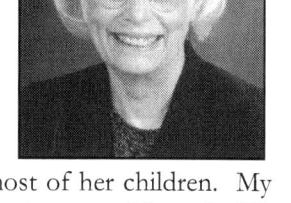

My mother was a stay-at-home mom, a bright lady, thank goodness. She passed that on to most of her children. My father was a bookkeeper, was in business, and later in life became the director of housing for the elderly in the city where I grew up, Central Falls, Rhode Island. I went to a parochial school which was run by the Sisters of St. Anne, who have Anna Maria College. Went through K [kindergarten] through 12, with the Sisters and then attended their college in Paxton [MA].

I was just happy to be a college student. I didn't really have any challenges to speak of. I enjoyed studying. I had a happy four-year experience in college. Met new, many new people, some of whom I have stayed in touch with. And I wanted to be a French major, and Anna Maria had an excellent French Department so that suited me fine. I was brought up bilingually which helps. I was brought up speaking French and I felt that was an advantage that I should make the most of. And so [I] continued, majored in French in college, went on for a Master's in French, and then taught for a few years at the high school level, and then went to France where I got my Doctorate at the University of Paris.

[I] spent ten years in France, in Paris, doing research for my Ph.D. And then doing research also on the Middle Ages out of which came a book ... a biography of Joan of Arc. So from Paris I came to Worcester, and have lived in Worcester since 1968.

I went to an all-girls school, [and] college. So that challenges were simply the rivalry of who was going to be the best student. But there have been challenges in life. Surely women still work much harder than men to get where, where they want to go. And there is the reality of the glass ceiling [that] is right there for all of us. We are living with it. You belong to a generation where some progress has been made, but someone said to me one day—he's a judge, and he said, "Claire if you belonged to a younger generation you probably would have become a judge just like me." But when I was looking at careers, what were the careers for women with a college education? Now if you had only a high school education, what did you become? A secretary, a nurse if you were lucky and your parents could afford to send you to nursing school, a bank teller; you know it was pretty limited. With a college education, teaching was usually where you ended up. But that was alright, I wanted to be a teacher so that was—that suited me fine. I was a high school teacher. Then after I got my Doctorate, I became a college professor—at the American University in Paris first where I also lectured, to different groups—American groups. And then when I came here [Assumption College], of course, I became—I started out as an Assistant Professor and moved on up to Associate and then to full Professor.

    My first year here, I must add, was difficult because they [the students] were still all- male. They were going to start accepting women the following year. And I remember when I first walked into one classroom, it was Intermediate French, and it was all boys, of course boys, men. And I could tell from their reaction that they thought Assumption had hit bottom, that Assumption College was really going to the dogs. They were against it; you know, the men who were here at the time did not want [the college] to accept women. And there was an inaudible groan, if I may put it that way, but you know, you don't hear anything, but you know [how they feel]. And it was in the gym, and it was a terrible place to teach besides. You know they had classrooms beneath the gym, so if they were rehearsing above, you heard the pounding of the balls. Let me say that that first year was interesting because I was teaching Intermediate French and I was also teaching a Senior Seminar. And the Senior Seminar went famously—again all men. And I enjoyed them, and I am still in touch with some of them. But the Intermediate French [class]—they didn't want to be there for one thing, you know when you really don't want to study French, but you have to because it was the rule at the time that you had to have so many semesters of a foreign language. And then to have a woman in front of you besides. So that was a humbling experience, and it was balanced, luckily, by the Senior Seminar. They were more mature, they were leaving anyway, they were not going to have to worry about having women in the classrooms with them. And then in the second semester, I began teaching at Clark [University]. And that was very important for me because the students at Clark were used to having women in front of them, you know as professors. Whereas here it had been all male. There is only one woman who preceded me here; she taught Russian. Madame Ziss was her name. So that the guys here were not used to having women teaching.

There was not much of a support system here at Assumption for women in those early years. For one thing there were some priests on the faculty and they had to be, they couldn't get too close to the women, because people would start gossiping. And the lay, the lay professors, well they had their own families to deal with and so forth. So let me just say that there was not much of a support system….But I am a fairly independent woman.

Ogretta McNeil
Age 78
Interviewed on: November 17, 2010 by Megan Evangelista, Britney Spencer, Katerina Reilly of Assumption College

I never even heard of Worcester, to tell you the truth. I didn't even know where it was; couldn't spell it nor pronounce it. I came here as a graduate student in 1956, and then I still went back for the next, the following two years and worked at the National Institutes for Health [in Bethesda, MD] in the summer because I, we were doing work on drugs and behavior. And also it gave me money, because I had no money. You know, in those days, you know, it was a whole different scene then it is now. And there certainly were no women and certainly no African-

American anybody—women or men—doing anything. When I was at the National Institutes for Health there was, I was—June and I were the probably the only ones. We were research assistants.

But you think about that, I mean I must have been crazy to do that. To come off to this foreign land in 1956. I didn't know where I was going and here's how it was introduced to me because I came on the train and you know you didn't have any money and I get in the cab and I tell the guy where I'm gonna live and he said, "I think you have the wrong address," and I said, "No I don't. This is where I'm going." He said, "No, you have the wrong address." I said, "Just take me there." And what I realized when I got in the cab he expected me to go to the African-American community, and I was living—I had an apartment over by Clark [University]. And I realized I was one of the only black people in that neighborhood. So you know it was a whole context, a whole lot of dynamics going on at the same time. And I could walk down Main Street and people would yell out of their kitchen, "Nigger!"

So, I came up here and that's it. I stayed here and believe me, I did, I just never imagined that I'd be here, in Worcester. But actually it grew on me and I actually met my first husband. He was a graduate student at Boston University getting his degree in Physics, Ph.D. [Doctor of Philosophy] in Physics.

And there were only two women in the class, and five guys. And so, this is interesting, this will give you the text of how life was then. I said to him when he asked me to marry him, "I don't know, I have to check with my—the chair of my department." And I think about it and I think, "Boy how things have changed." And he says, "What do you mean?" I said, "Well, you know, I mean, I can't do it if he tells me I can't." So, but anyway, fortunately [he] said yes. But I was scared!

It was just such a different environment when I think about it, and, and so few women. And certainly, very few African-Americans, male or female, who were going to graduate school. And actually I was the second African-American to receive a Ph.D. in Psychology from Clark [University] .... I got my degree in '67.

I didn't really know what it was I was supposed to be doing as a professional. Because there was—you know, who are your mentors, who was there for you to talk to? There was no one, really. Not a woman. And it was a male, a white male environment. And it was—it was a very competitive environment. Again I didn't know that.

But I was pregnant with my first son. Who was ... born in '61. And then in '63 the other one came along. And again, I—we—there [was] no planning, you know in those days. You guys [interviewers] plan everything. You know, you know, to the date. And I go, "I'm pregnant again? Wow, okay." And then, a year later, he was dead. So, I was a widow with two kids.

There are so many things that are available now that were not available then and I don't really know how I did it or why I did it, but it all worked out. The childcare was critical, if I had not had childcare I could not have done it. Especially during the time when I was doing my dissertation and I was running the experiment and she would drop him off and then I'd have different people including the chairman of the department babysit. I'd have someone doing my experiment and I'd hear my kids running up and down the hallway [laughs]. ... I had a lot of support ... from my classmates, from the faculty... It was a fabulous support system and I couldn't have done it without the support of my classmates, and other friends, and the community who really just pitched in and gave me that support.

[I] went to the College of the Holy Cross where I spent the rest of my career for about 27 or 28 years. It has not been an easy journey, but it has been an okay journey.

The reason it has been is because I have always had support and advocates, people who were there.

You have to have a supportive environment because you cannot do it by yourself. It really takes that and I've been really blessed to have a supportive environment both at home and in my community. My friends have been fabulous and I just couldn't have done it in a time that was so difficult, but it didn't mean the road wasn't difficult, because it was not an easy road for an African-American woman......... But I am glad that I decided to teach. It's been a very rewarding career for me. I met a lot of wonderful people on my journey and I'm glad that I chose this one. ...... But I can say this and I say this all the time to everyone: I have had an extraordinary life, a life that I never dreamed of.

Hilde Hein
Age 77
Interviewed on October 6, 2009 by Laura Cass of Simmons College

[I was born] in Cologne, Germany. I went to Berkeley High School. I became a Philosophy major at Cornell [University]. I had never heard of Philosophy. [Laughter] I had no idea. And so, I took Philosophy…and I loved it, and it was an easy choice for me; there was just no doubt. I fell in love with it, and that was it. So I went on in Philosophy, and just kind of one thing led to another and eventually [laughter] I ended up with a Ph.D. [Doctor of Philosophy] in Philosophy.

And then we came here [Worcester, MA], and I decided—by that time I had just had my third child, and I didn't—I thought I would stay home, but after three weeks of that, [laughter] I decided, "I don't think I want to stay home." And so I taught at Tufts [University] for a while, but that didn't lead to a full time job. And so then I went to [College of the] Holy Cross, which is how I ended up in Worcester.

I was the first one [female professor at College of the Holy Cross] to get tenured. Holy Cross went co-ed in 1972 which is the same year that Yale went co-ed. And it was a very exciting prospect. It didn't—just slowly it began to change the character of Holy Cross, but it didn't for a while.

I remember being asked in an elevator by one of the priests once, "What do they eat?" [Laughter] Seriously! So of course I responded, "Cottage cheese and rye crisps." There was a fear that the presence of women would mean that all sorts of unspeakable things would turn up in the plumbing system and there would be full length mirrors in the bathrooms and…. It was very strange.

I thought they were absurd, and I said so. [Laughter] I mean, I didn't go out on a campaign to prove that women were human beings, but—essentially I did I guess, by being…. It made a difference. Because it was very much an old boy network, and it was, you know, jokes told in classrooms which were unfit for female company and so…. I think the fear of what it would mean was real, and it turned out to only slowly become a reality because…. I think the first women by and large who were attracted to Holy Cross were the ones who would've gone to Catholic women's schools.

I taught a course on philosophers on women. Nobody would've thought of it [before going co-ed]. And actually the people who objected the most were not the faculty but the students. It was a very conservative bunch of students and they thought that this would just be a frill course. So I made it tough! I had them reading real philosophers. It was a very interesting lesson for me because I wanted to have women in the class, which meant that it had to be open to freshmen, because the only women who were there were freshmen, and so it had to be open enrollment. And so I got 75 students in that class, which—the majority were women, but the women were all freshmen and that upset the men in the class. Because—the women, because of their number and because the course was relevant to women, [it] sort of gave them a position of power. Well the men went berserk over that. And so I was really negotiating. I mean, you have to realize that this was something that was going on all over the country at that time. People—I mean, this was late '60s, early '70s—a lot of this kind of political exploration was going on, and so I was only doing what was happening everywhere else in my own eyes, but not in the eyes of either the administration or the students at Holy Cross.

I think that nobody expected women to achieve the level of representation, both on the faculty and among the students, their significance. I just don't think that anybody imagined that. I think that all of the schools that went co-ed at the time made that decision not motivated by human rights issues or equality issues, but largely financial issues because it increased the pool from which you could select students, and it meant that you could get better students.. But I don't think they understood—I don't think anybody understood—the qualitative change. "How is this going to impact what we actually do here?" I don't think…. I don't think they got it. And I think it has happened at Holy Cross as it happened everywhere else.

I think that for the first few years, what people said about women was essentially true: that the A students and the F students were going to be men, and in between there would be a range of women, and that was true. I had a lot of B students—women—not a lot of A students, and I think it was largely because they were shy, they were overshadowed by the men, and it was hard work to get them to open up, raise their hand, talk, have opinions because they weren't educated to do that, and it took a long time. And it took a kind of defiance of the norms, I mean, because you sort of had to almost violate them saying, "What do you think, Susan?" or "Miss so and so" or whatever it is I called them, [laughter] and that gradually changed over time, and I'm constantly aware of it even now. Young women now, more than older women my age, have a sense of entitlement. Of course the world is going to be there to provide their needs. That wasn't true then. It simply didn't enter into anyone's consciousness. And that did change over time.

I just don't think that we can relax and say, "Okay, we've done it, we're there." I mean I think that, right now, women are in a fairly good place, but I also don't want women to just become assimilated. I mean I think that we need to change the world, not become a part of it the way it is. And we're not there yet.

Laura Howie
Age 76
Interviewed on October 19, 2007 by Vanessa Taylor of College of the Holy Cross

I did go to Skidmore, as you know, and that was in '48 to '52. Where we went in the summer, there was a professor there and his wife and they were both professors [in the English Department at Skidmore] and so I had known them long enough. And then my mother and father had a very good friend who taught Biology. And she was there, so I think it was that way that I got steered that way to apply and so I did. I had four happy years at college in Saratoga Springs which was dead in the winter—it's not like it is now if you've ever been up there, but it was really dead in the winter. There was nothing because they just closed down—the college was the only thing there and it was really open in the summer racing season and everything.

It was my Home Economics people [that could be considered mentors]....so those professors and most of them were also housemothers. And I don't think of them as special mentors. I think that term has changed a little bit now .... But I did keep track of those professors because eventually Skidmore eliminated the Home Economics class, much to our disgust. Anyways, really it made a difference .... in my life and I did keep track of them afterwards. And I've been to just about all of my reunions, which is good, so I've gotten back there, even though it's changed and is a whole new campus and a whole new school.

I lived in Salisbury House, which was [the] one with the big pillars on the front. And there were only 32 of us in that particular dorm, so we got very close as far as that goes. And I mean, there were all different majors. And then I was in various other dorms. I chose a single room after that, and so, eventually I was in Skidmore Hall as a senior. And that's still there and being used as an apartment now, which is nice, it's just as you come up the hill..... And I just got a book from the last reunion that .... tells us all about it—describes the old houses and everything. I'm reading that, so you know, I am connected and I certainly made a lot of friends there .... I have happy memories.

Betty Hoskins
Age 72
Interviewed on November 13, 2008 by Lauren Carroccia
and Kerry Marasa of Assumption College

Women's colleges were formed usually by men or churches—mine was Methodist —to give women the opportunity to express their full selves, their intelligence, and their ability to bond with each other. And not all of the faculty were women, but there were spectacularly interesting and talented and famous women I had as an undergraduate. That's also true at Amherst for the men who are on the faculty. But the undergraduates were very bright and very sure that they would take very responsible positions in government and medicine and literature. But we were less sure of ourselves, we were much more tentative, and I'll give you one more. One of the college's slogans for raising funds, a campaign for funds while I was in college in 1956 was "Educate a man, you educate an individual. Educate a woman, you educate a family." And we believed it and we did it, but the whole notion of double tracking …. the whole notion of, "Mommy has enough money to stay home," that was normal. So, that was a difference, but it was even the same before college. It was the same with Boy and Girl Scouts, which I spent quite a few years in. You couldn't compete. And that was good for the culture, but it sure stifled a large part of us.

I lived for 19 years in Baltimore because I lived at home during college, because that was how to be frugal. That was true for my younger brother and younger sister too. And then I came—and here's my first at being an oddity—I came to Amherst College and did my Master's Degree. What's odd about it is it was then a male school, and a very highly prestigious male school. I didn't even ask, truthfully, I wanted to come here and do some research on how salamanders grow back an arm if it's bitten off or cut off. And I had worked on earthworm regeneration as an undergraduate and part of it was an interest in hormones, I won't go on about that now, but that became a theme and it got me a teaching assistantship at Amherst, and then I realized, "Oh my goodness, I'm the only woman [student] on campus." It was a very small graduate school but I was teaching undergraduates and it was a wonderful, enlightening experience because of what was expected of undergraduates there.

Then I married and moved to Dallas, Texas. I married a medical student and when he completed his M.D., we moved to Houston for his internship and also our daughter Catherine was born there, and then he—also having some good research experience—was invited to come to London, England, to do a post-doc [post-doctoral]. After London, my husband was invited to a post-doc in Stockholm, Sweden, in one of the labs that was doing early studies of RNA [ribonucleic acid] in cells. That means I was able to see the Nobel Prize awarded twice and go to the banquet. My son was born there. It was a very plummy time. We returned then to Dallas [sighs], well that was a tangled time, anyway it was interesting and useful. And eventually I got a job there teaching at a brand-new community college.

I decided I really needed to get my Doctorate, so I went racing off to Texas Women's College which is in Denton, near Dallas, but stayed living in Dallas. I did too fast the Doctorate and before I was even finished analyzing my data, I had asked my friends and my college advisor to look out for jobs and WPI [Worcester Polytechnic Institute], in the summer of '72, was looking for a woman. So I moved here [Worcester], and have stayed ever since.

I was invited to interview over the summer. And I said, "I'm not finished with my dissertation analysis, and I really can't come in the fall, the next month, plus the children need to be moved." And one was junior high, and one was, no, they were both in elementary school at Tatnuck. So they were very good, they said, "We'll hold the job until January." Which meant I arrived here moving back from Dallas with the dog, and the plants, and the children in the car and looked for a house. And they were really puzzled…WPI in general. [Imitating people's reactions] "You're coming to WPI? It's a boy's—men's school," but utterly welcoming. It was a curious experience and let me just preface, each college did their own way of going co-educational or integrating. [College of the] Holy Cross had hired a Dean of Women and started planning before they brought students. But WPI had had some applications from women, and my guess is they said, "Well, you know, no reason to turn them down, they're good," and then they said, "Oh my goodness, we need women's facilities." [Laughter] Originally, I was in a lab building which had no women's room so they had to designate one of the men's rooms. And there were grumbles like, "Oh, you know the secretaries didn't mind going to the next building, even in winter." Yeah, they'd put their coats on and walk through the snow to go to the bathroom. I said, "What's it coming to?" That's funny, in a way, but it's also, it meant that I got called "the one who's not smart enough to stay in her own department." Because I'm in the Women's Movement and was then ... I would get calls [imitates people questioning her], "We've been through the catalogue and we don't think there's much sexism but would you read it through for us?" And I had a feeling that I was not diplomatic and simply said something like, "If you know there's sexism in it, take it out, you don't need me." Or, "We're hearing that the women want shower curtains, do you think that's a reasonable expense?" On the one hand I was a part of an enormous change in society, on the other; it was very easy to accidentally end up with something, like, for instance, "She puts tension in the room when she chairs a committee." Well, there had never been a woman chairing a major academic committee there. It came up as something of, "Do we really want to retain her?" It was awfully hard on my family. They didn't really want to retain me, even though the faculty had accepted me as tenured. I think that was duplicated on every campus.

Linda Antoun Miller
Age 66
Interviewed on October 29, 2007 by Katelyn McDonald of College of the Holy Cross

My mother came here when she was 17 from Brazil to marry my father. Mom was, I think, quite an amazing woman in that she never had a college education, but she was self-educated. She read voraciously. She had an inquiring mind.

My father came here from Lebanon when he was seven. So, his formative years were spent there, but then he went to junior high and high school here in Worcester …. to Grafton Street Junior High and to North High and then he went on to college. He decided to become a doctor and went to Clark University for Pre-Med [Pre- Medical]. Then he went on to BU [Boston University] Medical School and post-medical education for surgery, University of Pennsylvania. So, he had a great value for education and my mother did because she didn't have it formally, although she was self-educated, so it was always assumed that the three of us would go to college. My brother went to Williams [College]. My sister went to Smith [College]. So, they set very high standards. I was the third; I went to Bates College in Lewiston, Maine.

It was understood that we would all have a liberal arts education. My parents felt that was very important, no matter what you did afterwards. Bates wasn't my first choice [laughs] to be very honest. I wanted to go to a small liberal arts college. My sister having gone to a girl's, women's school, my brother to a men's school, advised me to go to a co-ed college. At that time there was so many all-women's, all-men's colleges. But I received a fine education at Bates College. I met some classmates there who are still friends over 40 years later. The professors were excellent....It was sort of understood in my family that you went to college to study, to learn.... So, I pretty much kept my nose to the grindstone. I can't really say to you that I participated in a lot of activities at Bates. But I had been involved in many activities in high school and I wasn't attracted to them as much at college. I basically spent my time studying. I had a paid job in the library at the college and spent my time really pursuing my studies. And I had to study to achieve high grades.

But in junior year, I really wanted a bigger environment, and so I decided to enter the junior year abroad program, which they had just developed at Bates that year. I and two of my friends decided to go to England. We were all English majors. I went to Manchester in the north of England. It was a very positive experience for me being in a large university like Manchester and in a city as opposed to more rural Bates College in Maine. I think if I were to do it over again, I would have gone to a bigger university, but Bates was a fine small college and, I'd say I got a good education. It got me into Harvard Graduate School of Education [after graduating in 1963].

Harvard Graduate School of Education has a Master of Arts in Teaching program as did many universities such as Brown and Wesleyan. You could get a Master of Arts in Teaching in one year. You did six months academic courses and then six months in an internship at a regular teaching job that you shared with another intern. So, my partner and I shared a seventh grade English class at a junior high in Arlington, Massachusetts. I taught the first term while my partner did her coursework and then I did the coursework while my partner taught the class second term.

I taught for 27 years total. Middle school—eighth grade mostly. In my generation—and it was going to begin to change soon after—women didn't have all the options they have now. I didn't have all the options. My father wanted me and my sisters to be nurses, but we didn't want to do that. So, initially we both became teachers, and she went on to publishing from there and I remained a teacher.

When I first got into teaching, the Women's Liberation Movement had just begun. Betty Friedan had just written *The Feminine Mystique* and so I got into this. Well, I went to the library to get my son some books and I found books that said, "Men are pilots, women are stewardesses," "Men are doctors, women are nurses,"—very blatant sexism. Well, I went to the Holden Library and found these books and I raised the issue with the librarians at the same time and pointed this out. Even though I didn't have a daughter, it was important to me to show that girls could do anything. It was never suggested to me that I could be anything else but a nurse or a teacher. Or possibly a librarian…..Now in my life I see that I have strengths that suggest I could have been other things, not that I would have necessarily because I love to teach.

It's been such a learning experience to learn from one's students. I kept coming up with new ways. I liked creating new teaching units. For instance, I required my students to read books about women of courage. Many were being written during the mid-'70s to late '70s because of the new Women's Liberation Movement. And you learned all about these women you didn't know about who had done great things. That was exciting and some of my students … got really involved in this and learned a great deal from it… for the most part I had *wonderful* students.

Aida Gautier
Age 62
Interviewed on November 20, 2005 by Jose Encarnacion of Worcester State University

I was born in Puerto Rico in a town called Carolina, a village called Cambute. I remember it was countryside where you had farmers and horses. I was brought to the city at an early age, but I could remember the plants, the trees, the flowers. And in the city is where I went to school for my first grades. I was brought to New York City when I was eight and there is where I did all my schooling years and later on, I moved to Brooklyn, New York.

My mother tended to the house. We had a large family then—it was my mother, I had two brothers living with us, my sister—my sister was married at the time—and her baby. My mother used to take care of the baby. I would go to school and my brothers and my sister would go to work. That was the routine day—going to school, coming back from school, my family going to work. My mother would tend to the house, the cooking, and help around the house.

I finished my 12th year—I went through three quarters of the year because my mother passed away that October. I was already working part-time and going to school part-time. I could get the full-time job from where I was working part-time already and I asked my boss and he said it was okay. So I quit school and I was supporting my mother and my mother passed away that October and then I went to live with my sister and at a later point I finished school.

I was engaged when I was 18 and a half, 19 rather because after my mother passed away that is when we got engaged, and we got married a year after. We got married [in] 1965 in Brooklyn and I had four children with their father, and we moved to Worcester in 1972 and I had two more children from another.

One of my sisters-in-law came to visit Worcester with one of her relatives, and she came and she said that at that time it was very quiet. She came to Kilby Street and she told me she would like me to come to visit to see if I would like it and, indeed, I did. It was a very big change from New York City to Worcester in that year of 1971-1972 ... When I came to Worcester, once all my children were of school age I wanted to continue my schooling and I took the GED [General Equivalency Diploma] here.

I went to work part-time at the nursing homes because I had some children in school. And then when my daughter was old enough to go to daycare, when she was three years old, then I went to Quinsigamond [Community] College full-time and I did a year and a half. When she was having trouble with the provider, daycare provider she had, I figured I had to wait, that she would be older in order for me to finish school. So, that is what I did. I got a part-time [job] at the nursing home and I figured at some point I could finish school, but it was more important for me to make sure that she had a safe surrounding and I did so. I still haven't finished my schooling as I'd like to.

I took basic classes and I did the Allied Health that would gear me to the Nursing program. As a matter of fact, I was accepted into the Nursing program and that is when I started having problems with the daycare and my counselor told me that the Nursing program would be very hard and I would have to concentrate and having six children, raising them by myself, was not going to be easy. I was on the dean's list for one year—he used me as a model having six children and doing all the homework and that was great, but for the Nursing program, that was going to be hard. I was also accepted at the Atlantic Union College for the Nursing program, but again, I didn't have the adequate transportation and it was going to be very expensive. And not having someone reliable to take care of the children when they got out of school and to me that was important. So, I kept putting it off.

I would like to go back to school. I don't know if I would concentrate on the health activities and health sessions. But it would be nice to finish school, to have something complete. Complete something that I started that I wasn't able to finish. I always asked God to give the strength and the help. I had to do homework. I used to sit down when I had breaks by the grass where I used to live while waiting for the kids to come home from school...All I remember was going to school and church and I was carrying books here and there and everywhere. And I noticed the kids were doing the same thing. They used to play teacher and on the weekends they used to play church. That's what they saw me doing. So the image of parent is very important and I thank God that He gave me the strength. Without Him, I know that I could've never have done it, because He is the one that gave me the strength.

Donna Connolly
Age 53
Interviewed on November 11, 2009 by Gina Tremblay and Cori Schollard of Assumption College

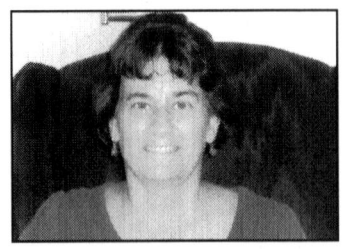

My father was Irish and Mom is Italian, but I feel like I identify more with the Italian side of the family, 'cause I grew up with my mom's side of the family, grandparents, and that kind of thing. I was one of five children, I was the oldest, and my dad died when I was 13. And a couple years later, my mom married a guy who had four children, so then there were nine of us!

I grew up as I said, very close to my grandparents and my mom's side of the family. It was pretty rough growing up because my father wasn't healthy at all… and as the oldest one I think the burden of a lot of things came upon me, and I watched my mom struggle a lot. She got married very, very young, and then had children …. that's what you did in those days, and [she] really hadn't worked much outside of the home. And so, I think what all that taught me was that you need to be able to do things on your own and make sure you have a career, get an education, have a career, so that you can take care of yourself if that needed to be. And I think that probably the best part of my life was when I was a teenager, when mom remarried and I had this—got a bunch of more brothers and sisters, and that was a good thing for all of us, and continues to be. My parents are both still living and they both had a second chance at a new life, and we all did, so it was a good thing!

I think using my mom as an example, she graduated from high school, worked for a little bit, and had her first child at 19, was married, so, you know, she said there weren't a lot of options available to you. She never saw herself as going to college, but that didn't seem to be something that people did. So not really having a career, and then you know, her role was to take care of the home, take care of children, no matter what was going on, and obviously that's very, very different, and knowing that, I think that getting an education is key to getting yourself moving. So it's very different now, and I can't imagine not having my children or my nieces going to college. I mean that's a given, or having a career that they can take care of themselves in. I knew I wanted to go to college. I always loved school. I was a good student. I felt like it actually came pretty easy to me. I liked it. I liked what I was taking so there wasn't a lot of challenges there. Schoolwork was like something that I could do and that I felt like I was good at.

I really loved it here [Assumption College]. I have made, I made a great group of friends and, in fact, this past weekend I was on the Cape [Cod] with my, my "Assumption Girls" as I call them. There's seven of us that go away at least once a year and you just feel like these are women that I really bonded with, but we're different, we live in different places, we've had different experiences as far as marriages or anything else, but when push comes to shove these are people that I can count on in my life. So, it was a great thing here. I loved watching basketball—[it] was really big at the time. I'd, we'd always go to the games, that kind of thing, and some of the other sports too, 'cause you had friends playing and you know, the girls volleyball team or softball or something like that that you do. So sports was a big part of watching things here. I did intramurals when I was here. Worked [in] what's now below the gym. There was a snack bar down there. Flipping burgers and stuff like that.

There were more men than women at the time here. It had just been in the, what, the late 1960s when it turned over, so it wasn't 50-50, but it was probably getting close to that because they were accepting more women at the time, so it's not like it is today, where there are more women on campus than men.

I work for the Colleges of Worcester Consortium. I work there on a federal grant out at one of the high schools here in Worcester, South High. I work with low-income, first generation college students. So, my focus is with kids who need extra help, with their families who may not be familiar with the whole college process. I have a lot of immigrant students, or families who are immigrants, so they came here looking for a better life, from many, many different countries, and helping them with the whole college process, the financial aid process, filling out the FAFSA [Free Application for Federal Student Aid] forms, doing all that stuff. And I've been at South High for 14 years. This is my fourteenth school year there.

[Advice I would give women of today and future generations would be to] do what you want to do first, before you settle down. Don't let that guy dictate what you're doing. I see in the high school that I'm at, I see young girls who really get caught up and say, "Oh well I need to do this because my boyfriend really wants me to do that," or, "He doesn't want me to go away to college." Oh please. You know? This is not a reason to pick a college. I think really making sure you know who you are, what you want to do, you have some skills to be able to take care of yourself if you're ever going to need that, and never let somebody have that kind of control over you.

For me it really is about giving others an opportunity to have what I had and not, maybe not having the support at home, not because parents don't want to, but maybe they just can't give it for whatever the reasons might be. So making sure that they can have an education, have a career that they can also be giving back. So it really is about giving back. I never thought I'd be working with high school students. If you had said that to me when I was at Assumption I would have said, "Oh no way! There's just no way!"

Brenda Safford
Age 52
Interviewed on March 30, 2009 by Hannah Brencher
and Julie Perry of Assumption College

I attended high school in Lubbock [Texas]. I had a skill. I could type. And you have to remember, this was before the computer world. We had the manual typewriter and I could type 90 words per minute with three errors. So I was like a human machine. So that allowed me to get into a position of being well paid for the work I could do. So when I married my husband and went into the military work world, they loved that about me. What happened to me though, when I came here to Worcester, I developed rheumatoid arthritis in my hands. So I became completely disabled. They told me, "You should go to college," and at that point I was like 38.

So I thought, "It is over for me. I can't, are you crazy? I can't go to school now." And they said, "Why not?" And that is how I began my educational journey as a late learner, an adult learner. And I went on to Quinsig [Quinsigamond Community College], and then I came here –they gave me a scholarship. I came to Assumption [College] and got my Master's Degree.

I was able to figure out that when I was going to my high school as far as integration, they took all of our prominent teachers and sent them over to the white schools. And the white schools sent over student teachers. Not teachers, but student teachers. There was remorse like, "I cannot teach these kids anything." So I think in my education, I was failed. Because I didn't get 100 percent from the teachers. And this is what happens to people. You know we have a federal law protecting us and civil rights. It is going to happen, and integration is going to happen, but you can't change the people's hearts. You can change the laws, but you can't change hearts. And I think that was a really unfortunate thing, not only for me, but for that high school that year and all the kids.

I went from clerical typist to the name being changed to administrative assistant. And in El Paso, Texas, there was this huge corporation called the El Paso Natural Gas Company. And because of my typing skills I was able to get in. And when you get in, that was supposed to be *the* job and a great job for women. And I loved it. It was [pause] an eye-opening experience and I learned a lot from it. And I was really proud because my reputation was that I was really good. And every time someone was looking for a new person to set up, I was always there. Every time we relocated I always could find a job, always, always. I worked as an EKG tech [electrocardiogram technician]; I worked always as a secretary. And when I first came here [Worcester] too, I worked at Guaranty Bank. I just don't like bank work; I know that is not my cup of tea. But I went to this place, this corporation that, it is called the Melville Corporation that is incorporated with CVS [Consumer Value Store], Tech Team, all those stores. I was in the human resource department. So they gave me 600 stores nationally. And I had to do hiring, termination, vacation, union dues, everything. And I was very good until the company went bankrupt. And then, that's when I went to the Worcester Public Schools and I worked for the School Committee. And actually when I first started working there was the time that Senator Harriette Chandler, she was on the school committee with me. And she just sort of found a connection with me and she always told me, "You should go to school."

And Dr. Caradonio [Superintendent of Worcester Public Schools] came in and he was impressive. And I went into his office and said, "Do you want me to set you up? I can, I can come over," and I completely developed his office. And we got to talking and he was the one that first kind of planted the seed of education by saying, "You should really go to college and get your degree, Brenda." And I kept saying that I was too old and he would say, "Hogwash! Go!" And he started giving me all these points and I looked at him like… and ironically maybe three or four months down the road that's when I really started school, but he was there for graduation. And when I graduated from here Channel 5 came, the [Colleges of Worcester] Consortium [through Ed Central] had done a movie on me.

It was big! But I was saying, "You should not use me, go use the younger people." But they laughed and told me I ought to think about what I had done and that I could show other women that you can do this at any age. And I never did look at my stuff like that, personally, until that day.

The key thing in my story is that I stepped up to the challenge of going to school as an adult learner. I could have said, "No, no, no, no. I give up and this is it. I will just be on disability and I can get retrained to do another job." But the ability that I had to accept that challenge, I think that is where the learning and the teaching come from, of doing that. But I do want people to know of accepting the challenge in life. Sometimes we have to do that, even if we have fears. Step to the challenge and say, "Yes I can. I can do this," or "I can try." Because we don't know if we are going to succeed when we step to the challenge, but we will try.

Nancy Caruso
Age 51
Interviewed on October 18, 2006 by Meghan Caruso of Worcester State University

  In my day and age—I graduated in 1973—we had three choices: we either could be a nurse, we could be a teacher, or we could be a secretary. In my high school, if you were to be a secretary, then you were tracked in the business tracking, and I was too smart for that they said. So, it was really a choice of being a nurse or a teacher. Who was instrumental into getting me into the teaching field? [That] was my sister and guess what? She's a Home-Ec [Economics] teacher, too. I would see the kinds of things she was doing. I should also say that my mother went to Girl's Trade [High School] and she was a stitcher. So, we kind of had that home-ec thing in us anyway, but I really liked what she was doing and I was cut out to do the same thing.

  I teach at South High School in Worcester. It is one of the more difficult schools to teach in. I have been there for—let me think—22 years. It is an open-classroom situation and that's why it's difficult to teach there. And what that probably means [laughs] for those who are unknowing—in the 1970s in California, they came out with this wonderful new educational concept. And that is to have what's called pods. So the areas where ... four or five teachers ...will be teaching in the area and there are no walls. So, it can be noisy, especially since I teach in an area where it's culinary arts.

The students in school come from a very low economic background. There's a lot of gang-related kinds of stuff happening in the community – we do have a gang unit on call at the school. We are the only school in Worcester who's had the distinction of having somebody stabbed there and killed back in the '80s. As long as the teachers are on board in understanding what their role is, as far as discipline, it's an okay place to work in. I do not feel unsafe in the school. I also happen to teach in an area where the kids elect to take my course rather than told they have to take my course. So is it challenging? Is it difficult? Yes. It's also very many situations where they do not speak English. Our school represents 52 different countries and a variety of languages. So, yeah, very challenging.

Brenda Gordon
Age 48
Interviewed on October 15, 2006
by Andrea Kohl
of Worcester State University

I first came to Worcester in, I believe it was 1965. I think I was about seven then, and I moved, we moved to Forest Street. And I lived there until I graduated from high school, which was about ten years later or so, and I moved out on my own with some girlfriends.

I remember walking to grammar school. We would walk—it was Nelson Place Grammar School, Elementary School—we would walk there and we would walk home for lunch too, so I really remember that—the back and forth. We'd have lunch and go back for the rest of the day. It's probably my earliest [memory]…..I'm not really sure what grade, if that was second grade or probably a little bit older from what I remember.

I remember when I went to grammar school, at least early on there, girls always used to wear dresses or skirts and I remember we could wear pants under our skirts when we'd walk in snowy conditions and we could put pants on. We'd have to take them off once we got to school—we'd have our dress on. But that changed. I don't really remember what year that was, when we were allowed to wear pants to school, but it was sometime during that time. Maybe I was sixth grade by then or something. Now at Forest Grove [Middle School] I still walked to school—I could walk there—it was really close to my house. I remember it being kind of a confusing time.

In high school….we'd have to take the bus…. so, we'd walk down to the corner and a school bus would come and we'd take the bus to school there and that was—I remember it being better. I liked it more…. it just seemed to offer more of the things you were really interested in as far as that goes. ….. High school you could pick and choose a little bit more of the classes you wanted so it was a good time. I think it was a typical high school experience for me. You know, you had your groups of kids: the jock, the drug kids, smoking kids, you know—the real smart kids. I don't think much has changed in high school.

I was a very good student. I was in the quiet, just let me do my work and go home [group], but I was in a lot of business classes so I loved it 'cause that was—I just liked all that kind of stuff. Typing and shorthand and then we did business machines. What is shorthand? [Laughs] Wow, isn't that funny? Shorthand was a shortened way of writing phrases and sentences. So, like in the old days when you had a boss and you were a secretary and they wanted to dictate a letter, you would be taking it down in shorthand to keep up with what he was saying to you. Then you would type it out, you'd transcribe it back. You know now we have these little machines that record your voice and then you go back and type them. So, it was like another language, but it was fun, very interesting.

What I hoped to do with it was if I got into a company where I was a secretary—which was sort of a goal at the time—I could take down a letter that way. That was how you had to do it.....I liked office stuff. I just always liked the stuff that goes with the office.....I didn't really consider at all going to college because I just thought I'd work in an office someday which would have made me really happy....The only thing that maybe I would have liked to do was go to a college that specialized in business or, you know, secretarial stuff, maybe doing legal transcribing.

Probably many of the kids in my class did go on to college.... But I think just for me I, I didn't have college in my mind to do. Part of it probably was my older sister—who's kind of the same way as me—liked the business aspect of things and the secretarial part and sort of did the same typing and stuff that I did. And my parents didn't have a lot of money so they weren't really talking to us or pushing us to go to college..... I knew she didn't go, so I think maybe it was probably the same for me. I can get a job and be happy doing that, and ... I can't afford to go to college.

Claire Constantin
Interviewed on March 6, 2008 by Pat Doherty of College of the Holy Cross; ASL Interpreter, Betty Filipkowski

I became deaf when I was three years old. At first, my father did not accept it. I wasn't able to speak and he did not allow me to sign. So I had to learn how to speak all over again, and that took about two or three years, and finally my father started to accept it, but he wanted me to stay involved with the hearing world, and [I] stayed within the hearing world until I was about ten. That did not work and I did eventually transfer over to a deaf school in Boston. But I did go to a hearing high school. But still my parents never accepted me fully as a deaf person and did not learn to sign.

The hearing schools were more difficult. Deaf schools were easier, but I think if I had an interpreter it would have been much easier for my education, but it was hard without the interpreter. My friends would actually help me out in school by taking notes for me and I would sit up front in the classroom and watch the teachers so I could read their lips. But it was difficult.

It would be really nice if the hearing people could understand the deaf people more, for communication, I think that's what needs to change. A lot has changed [in Worcester]; we have interpreters now. We have a lot of deaf services such as the Mass Rehab [Massachusetts Rehabilitation] Commission. We have the Massachusetts Commission for the Deaf and Hard of Hearing. We have the Center of Living and Working, the Senior Center—there's so many services now, not like it was a long time ago.

My experiences and being involved in the Deaf community it's—I really like to help and work with the Deaf community. I like being the coordinator here at the Senior Center.

Guillermina Elissondo
Interviewed on April 14, 2006
by Jenna McNulty and Michael Carpentier of Worcester State University

I was born in Argentina in a place called

Tandil. I think a few teachers I had in high school really had a lot of intellectual influence on me. I come from a culture where we don't really have the notion of role models, that's an American thing I think. I always think about this one teacher because I really respected her intellectual abilities. She was a really nice person. She taught History. I went to the Catholic University of Argentina and did my undergraduate in English then I got my Master's Degree at Michigan State, and my Ph.D. [Doctor of Philosophy] in North Carolina.

I was 26 [when I moved to the United States.] My husband got a Fulbright Scholarship and we came for a year. It was in the middle of a dictatorship and when you have a Fulbright Scholarship, you need to return to your country for two years. So, we went back and things were really bad for the country and we decided to come back here.

First I worked—because I didn't have the papers to go back to school—I worked in a factory. In Argentina, I never had to do that type of job. I couldn't afford anything else at the time though. Then I wanted nothing to do with Spanish. I wanted to take English courses. Then I realized if I stayed here, I couldn't study much. So, I applied for the Master's in Second Language Acquisition and I got an assistantship in Spanish. And that's how I paid for it.

From Michigan, we moved and my husband taught in Pennsylvania and then I lived in North Carolina. At the time, I was teaching at a college in North Carolina. My boss, he was the vice president, and he really encouraged me to go for my Ph.D. And then the college gave me a paid leave of absence for a year, a salary for me to pay for the classes at the university and that year I finished the coursework. Then I went back to work and at night I wrote my thesis—400 pages. I used to get up at 1:00 in the morning and write until 5:00 a.m.

[When] I did my undergrads in English ... well, in those years it was very difficult to afford.... it was even difficult to mingle with native speakers. Mastering the language here was a tough time. Also in those years, the intellectual part was not very important because those were years during the military dictatorship—the '60s and the '70s—and political projects were much more important than intellectual progression for the college. Then when I came here, it was kind of—I was taking courses in a Master's level in English and you're surrounded by all native speakers and the papers are all in English and I think that when I got into the Master's it was something I studied in Argentina—it was easy for me.

Then when I got into the Ph.D., I didn't want to do the Ph.D. in Spanish. My Ph.D. is in Education because I didn't want to do Literature. I'm interested more in Cultural Studies. So, I did my thesis on Education and Cultural Studies. And the whole Ph.D. was in English. I had to write all my papers in English. I had to write my dissertation in English. I was the only non-native in the class—they were all American. So, nobody came from my background in foreign languages. So, it was tough. I was also working full-time and I had a child so, you know I think ... I couldn't do it now! It was tough. And I didn't have anybody. Anybody. My husband, who was also writing and trying to get published ... so those were very difficult years of my life, getting my Ph.D.

I think that we [women] have a much easier way than they did in the past. I don't think that in my personal experience, in my situation, that things are so bad. But I do think that when I think of this society, or when I look at the society in Latin America, it's different. It's pretty bad. Women are working a lot more now. They are leaving the home, but the top jobs in the corporations are not held by women. Those jobs are handled by men. I'm not concerned with middle class women's situations as much really. It's more the lower class I think. Women who have no education, women who are abused by the system. They have no education; they have issues with domestic violence. Those are things that I think have seriously improved in the middle class and upper class levels, but are still problems in the lower class. Women should have education. That's the real solution to the problem. Education.

CHAPTER THREE

WORK

"The number of her industrial avocations are unnecessarily restricted, far more than reason demands. And when she is engaged in the same occupations with men, her remuneration is greatly below what is awarded to her stronger associates."

> Abby H. Price—Proceedings, October 23, 1850, afternoon session of the First National Woman's Rights Convention

Work may be defined as exertion or effort directed to produce or accomplish something. While this is true, this is hardly the full explanation. Ask a group of ten individuals to explain what work is, and you will probably receive 11 definitions. There is paid labor and unpaid labor. There is work that brings home a paycheck, and there is work that feeds the soul. Work is often connected with issues of self-esteem, allowing individuals to make use of special abilities, skill, and knowledge. While it can provide money, it can also allow one to contribute to the community in meaningful ways. It can foster creativity and give one a sense of power over one's life.

So what has work meant for women, specifically the women of Worcester? For many, its meaning and significance have changed over time. When Abby H. Price addressed the First Woman's Rights Convention on the afternoon of October 23, 1850, she used these words:

> …in many countries we see women reduced to the condition of slave, and compelled to do all the drudgery necessary to her lords' subsistence. In others she is dressed up as a mere plaything, for his amusement; but everywhere he has assumed to be her head and lawgiver, and only where Christianity has dawned, and right not might been the rule, has woman had anything like her true position…The natural rights of woman are co-equal with those of man…They were both made in the image of God…they are absolutely equal in their rights to life, liberty, and the pursuit of happiness…Therefore each has equal right to pursue and enjoy it [happiness]. This settled, we contend:
>
> 1. That women ought to have equal opportunities with men for suitable and well-compensated employment.
> 2. That women ought to have equal opportunities, privileges, and securities with men for rendering themselves pecuniarily independent.
> 3. That women ought to have equal legal and political rights, franchises, and advantages with men.

Historically, being a wife and mother were often regarded as the primary professional goals for women. Frequently considered the weaker sex, jobs requiring strength and stamina were not open to female applicants. Of course, this line of reasoning ignored the fact that strength was needed by women to milk cows, plow fields, give birth, and care for vast numbers of children.

In early colonial America the work of women most often centered on the home. Many wives worked side by side with husbands to establish farms. In 1800 nearly 80 percent of all Americans worked on farms. With few labor saving devices available, food preparation was very time consuming and accounted for a major portion a wife's day. The spinning of yarn, the weaving of cloth, and the sewing and mending of clothes occupied much of a woman's time as well.

With the advent of the Industrial Revolution during the 1840s and 1850s, many left farm life, seeking work in shops and mills. This new working class was comprised of a great many women in search of a better life. While some may have found fulfillment of their hopes and aspirations, many found disappointment and disillusionment. Women and children were paid lower wages than men, so factory owners were often happy to hire them. Women toiled in factories, worked as shop girls, or taught school. These women all shared a common bond. Their salaries were far less than those paid to men.

Women's opportunities for work increased dramatically during the 20th century. The vote was won in 1920 and that milestone had repercussions that are still resounding today. When the U.S. entered World War I, the workplace opened its doors to women. Women filled the jobs that had previously been held by men. During World War II, thousands of women again entered the workforce, taking the places of men who were fighting overseas. Many of those women gave up those jobs and paychecks when the men returned from battle.

Challenges for women in the workplace continued into the mid-20th century. Help Wanted sections of newspapers were often clearly delineated into Help Wanted Male and Help Wanted Female. The female job opportunities were usually categorized as housekeeping, secretarial, nursing, and teaching positions. If a man and woman worked at the same job, it was not unusual for the man to be paid a higher wage. That all changed with Title VII and the Equal Pay Act. Title VII states that it is illegal for any employer "to fail or refuse to hire or discharge any individual with respect to his compensation, terms, conditions, or privileges of employment because of an individual's race, color, religion, sex, or national origin." At last the advertisements simply read Help Wanted.

The Equal Pay Act states that employers are required to pay men and women equally for comparable work. Comparable jobs do not necessarily mean identical jobs. Two jobs would be considered comparable if their value to the business was equal and both jobs required equal skill, effort, responsibility, and working conditions. While this hardly seems a revolutionary concept by 21st century standards, there were many who lodged complaints that this law was unfair to men who needed to support families.

Challenges still exist in the workplace of the 21st century. As you read the stories of contemporary Worcester women in these pages, perhaps you will identify and empathize with their struggles and their achievements. Life in the modern world can be complex and difficult to navigate. It can also be rewarding and fulfilling. While today's women may contemplate a variety of careers compared to the choices available to their mothers or grandmothers, problems and injustices still exist in the workplace. The glass ceiling, the effort to balance work and family time, sexual harassment, and gender wage discrepancy are real obstacles encountered by working women in this country. In this chapter you will encounter an immigrant from Nigeria dedicated to her work with the homeless, an artist who is the mother of six, a young Episcopalian priest, and many others who are pursuing goals about which previous generations of women could only dream. As women persevere, they can find courage and inspiration in the words of Susan B. Anthony, "Cautious, careful people, always casting about to preserve their reputation and social standing, never can bring about a reform. Those who are really in earnest must be willing to be anything or nothing in the world's estimation."

Genevieve Irene Lucier
Age 90
Interviewed on October 22, 2006 by Charlotte Zax

I've enjoyed every decade of my life because they're all different and interesting. And I've never minded going from one decade to another. I'm having a fine time in my nineties.

My mother was born in Hudson, Massachusetts where she lived all of her life until she came to Worcester after my mother and father were married. She was an at-home person. But when I was five years old and just starting school, she decided she would like to do some hairdressing in the home. So she went to some lady who would teach her hairdressing. I was able to come home from school and have lunch at a neighbor's home, so my mother knew I was taken care of. And when she received her license, she did hairdressing in the home. In those days they did curling iron curls and then waves in the hair with combs, and wet combs, and things like that. And she enjoyed doing it. We had three bedrooms, consequently she had a room in which she could do this, because there was just the three of us. My parents had a room, I had a room, and this other room was her hairdressing parlor.

My father thought it would be a fine idea if I worked in an office. I listened to my father. I didn't know anyone in my immediate area who was going to college, and it didn't occur to me, so I worked in an office. When I graduated in 1933, no one thought of getting a job, because you were lucky at that point if your father had a job. My father had a job, and he was the kind of man who would find one if he didn't have one. He didn't have a lot of money, but we had a meal every day. I didn't suffer by any means.

My father was a janitor at the *Telegram & Gazette* and he found out that that the paper was hiring girls who could type. It was a temporary thing. I was hired in September and worked there until December. Then I went back to school at Commerce High for post-graduate courses to hone my skills. And the school sent me out on temporary jobs. I went to work for the Chamber of Commerce for a couple of months. Then I went to Baker Lumber. They were doing a new price book. I was typing on that project.

In the meantime, my father said, "Go down to the agency in Worcester every day and apply for a job. When there is one, they'll know that you're looking for one." I did what my father said. He had very good ideas. I never felt that he was pushing me into anything. He was a very, very smart man without an education. The day came when I received a call from that employment agency. I was to go to Standard Brands, which was out opposite Our Lady of the Angels Church, on Main Street. So I went there. You can imagine how many there were. I was 18, I graduated when I was 17. I wore my most grown-up looking dress and gloves. I was interviewed and I got the job. I worked for that company for 19 years, some of them being in the Boston office.

My parents were getting older and I thought I should come back to Worcester. They needed me here, and I went to work for the Paul Revere Insurance Company. I spent the rest of my working life there, 28 years. Then I retired from there.

I had a friend who was a member of the Music Guild. She kept encouraging me to join. I said, "When I retire in 1981, I'll join because all of your events are in the daytime." Then my friend became president of the guild in 1980 and I thought, "Why don't I join now and make her look good?" So I did that. I went to the first event in September of that year. I went to the first lecture, and I was hooked. I just loved it, and I've never stopped loving it since.

In 1981 I became co-chairman of hospitality for the Music Guild. I took care of this for the next two years. Then I was asked to be treasurer. I said, "Fine." That was in 1984, and I'm still treasurer after 22 years. I'm not interested in the computer. I use eight and one-half by eleven notepads. I do my treasurer reports on that, and they look fine. I make photocopies for the meetings and I do the mailings as well.

I always say that I find all eras of my life to be interesting and good. I've enjoyed them all. When I worked at Paul Revere, I worked with several young ladies. When they would turn from 29 to 30, they would be holding their foreheads. I would say, now every age is good, something different. And they would say, "She's put on the record again." This is true. So, that's the way I've always felt. It's not too bad to get old. Who wants to be one age all the time? I liked them all. I'm enjoying being 90.

Mildred Louise Beams Cummings
Age 78
Interviewed on April 5, 2008 by Stephanie Camerlengo and Arta Gjemnicia of Assumption College

I was born during the Depression. My father worked in carpet mills and that wasn't a good profession at the time, but it was a steady job. My mother worked as a clerk in a bakery downtown in Worcester. When the war started in 1941, my father got a job at Heald Machine Company. This was a better job. I know he was trying to join the service, but he got turned down because of his heart condition.

I remember having a babysitter when I was in grammar school. In 1938 a massive hurricane hit the city and my parents were at work. My aunts lived across the street and I went there. I remember my father coming home. He and my uncle went across the street to where we lived to check on our house. I remember my mother getting home later and by then it was rainy and windy and stormy. We spent the night at my aunt's house. And, of course, the next morning the sun came out. This happened in September, and we were out of school for a week.

When I was in high school, I was a babysitter for a little boy. I received 15 cents per hour, two dollars per week, and we thought that was fantastic. When I was a little older, 16 or 17, I worked in a dairy doing bookkeeping.

I went to nursing training at Memorial Hospital. This was something I always wanted to do. We weren't poor, but we weren't rich. So, I did go to nursing school on a scholarship. It was four hundred dollars a year. I really enjoyed nursing. Because of the scholarship, I had to work at the hospital for a year after I graduated.

I worked at the hospital until I was seven months pregnant, then I stopped working to raise my kids. Later, I went back to work part-time. I worked three to eleven. My husband was going to barber school, so he went to school during the daytime, and I worked three to eleven.

There was never a question about working while I was pregnant. You had to quit at a certain time in the pregnancy. You didn't get maternity leave. But it wasn't a problem. I was married and my husband had a job. And then later when I returned to work part-time, I had a young teenaged friend of ours come to the house as a sitter.

My husband had several odd jobs before he went to barber school. But then he bought a barbershop in Millbury, and then we started a barbershop in Auburn. I looked after the kids and I worked, and my husband was a barber. He worked from eight in the morning until six or seven at night. The children and I learned to work together. We did lots of things together—repairs, painting, mowing the lawn, and all kinds of yard work.

Two of the best things I ever did in my life was becoming a nurse and learning to drive. And I learned to do them before my husband died. I was working full-time as a nurse, which was my saving grace, because I was able to keep my family and raise my kids. When I went back to nursing, I was making $3.75 an hour and when I retired in 1995, I was making $15.75 an hour. It was enough for me to raise my family. When my husband died unexpectedly, my sister and her husband came to our rescue, too. My youngest was only 12 when her father passed away.

Maureen Barbara McLaughlin
Age 75
Interviewed on April 14, 2006 by Christopher Antaya of Worcester State University

Until I was 24, I lived in Worcester. Since my marriage, I have lived in Millbury. That's 51 years. When I was in school, I loved math and geography. I hated physics, but I loved to read. I spent my Saturdays at the library. I would gather all the books and sit in the library all day Saturday, because we didn't have that many books at home. I still love to read.

I really wanted to be a schoolteacher, but we didn't have the finances. So, I became a nurse. Back in those days, I don't think women had many options like they have today. You either worked in a factory, became a secretary, or schoolteacher, or nurse, or got married.

I always worked and I paid for my nursing education after high school. From the time I was eight or nine, I worked. I had a paper route. I got up in four in the morning and delivered papers at eight years old. My brother had one route and I had the other. We used to meet in the middle and come home together. On Sunday it was the *Sunday Telegram* route and we used wagons. The Sunday paper was so heavy that we had to carry them around in wagons.

When I was about 12 years old, I got a job working at a farm stand on Moreland Street. I sold vegetables there until I was about 16. At 16 I got a job at a grocery store on the lower end of Main South. I would go there after school. I was there until I went to nursing school. I did babysitting in-between. The money wasn't that much. At that time papers were only 24 cents a week. The customer would give you a quarter and they would want the penny back. You didn't put the papers in the mailbox. Everybody wanted them delivered to their door. So I developed a strong arm folding those papers and throwing them up on the third floor porches of the three-deckers in Worcester.

I stopped working as a nurse about a year after I got married. It was a three-year nursing program and then I worked for about two years afterward. My husband owned his own gas station and I did all the bookkeeping and billing for his business. And I had six children. They occupied all my time.

I think women in the past were too passive. They didn't speak up. We were too limited. I'd say now go for anything they can get. I mean, the choices are so big for women. Years ago, men ruled the roost, believe me. Women were supposed to stay home and keep their mouths shut, but today women can do so many things. Just go for it.

Sr. Carol Skehan
Age 68
Interviewed on November 13, 2008
by Lauren Trapasso of Assumption College

I came here, I had just turned 14. And you know, you're filled with enthusiasm and you want to serve God…That's what I did and let me tell you, the novitiate was like boot camp. I am sure that any of us could have gone into the Marines [United States Marine Corps] with no trouble…It was tough emotionally, the rules, the discipline…it was an intense indoctrination.

[My father] bought me a scooter. I was here [teaching at Venerini Academy], but I hated scooters They only go 32 miles per hour…and people would get mad—you were going too slow. Then I got a bigger scooter and I rode all over. We rode… my father, my niece and nephew, and myself. We'd go to New Hampshire to flea markets. But you can't buy much when you're on a motorcycle…So I had an opportunity to get a motorcycle from someone…for three hundred dollars. I was scared stiff. I had never driven shift, so I went to a safety class.

Some of the older nuns…never said anything, but I know they complained. I heard them one time…Yes, well I never took to rules that well. It's amazing I entered the convent. Let me tell you, it's a miracle. I live on the edge of the rules. They call me a maverick, I'm like McCain [U.S. Senator John McCain], but I'm not a Republican.

Over the years when the Charter [Charter Communications] first started, cable companies, we had cable on one TV because at that time it was against the law to put more TVs in your house. Now we had 26 bedrooms. I wired the whole side of my house for TVs…Going through the heating system with my drill…That was illegal but I did it anyway, and I didn't tell the nuns you couldn't do it! I hope I won't be arrested for this.

I've been teaching about 46 years…I taught first grade for 14 years…Probably a reason I like the little kids, too, because you can be the boss…I was never radical. But I think we need radical people, because radical people make the rest of us think, and they do gutsy things that the rest of us are scared to do. So, I'm grateful that there are radical feminists 'cause they made the way for the rest of us...A lot of people don't realize, but we want to have women priests! And there are a lot of women speaking up and doing things that the bishops don't like...

If you can die...and it can be said that you lived a good life and were kind and kids loved me, that's what I'm happy with...So I think if you leave an impact on a child...they remember. They remember the kindness and they remember the one time you yelled at them! But if you can be remembered for being kind and loving, that's what I want to be remembered as. Put that on my tomb...I'm actually going to be cremated and have my ashes thrown in the woods. I don't even know if that's allowed, but that's what I want done. But why shouldn't that be done?

Kathleen O'Connor
Age: 61
Interviewed on March 14, 2011 by Andrew Harmon and Nathan Masse of Assumption College

I was a teacher first—as my first profession—and I moved to Florida in 1974. I taught there, then I went to Philadelphia to go to law school, and practiced law there for two years after law school. And then I decided to come home!

I went to Worcester State [University] because I was going to be a teacher. And I think this is one of the things that was very different at that time...for women. The educational and career opportunities were pretty limited—or at least we were *told* that they were limited...My father told me when I was five years old that I was going to Worcester State, so I just did.

I had only taught for five years and I had never imagined doing anything different than teaching. But in my fifth year of teaching, I became very interested in the union activity that was going on among the teachers...We ended up on strike. It was an illegal strike, by the way, and I participated in it just like everyone else, and I got very interested in the union functioning, and I realized I wanted more education. It occurred to me one day that I might want to be a lawyer after watching the lawyers work on the union issues regarding the strike. But I wanted to tie the law into education, because I still loved everything about education. So I looked for a law school that had a labor activity. I ended up in Temple Law School in Philadelphia, and I got exactly the experience that I wanted. I worked with the Philadelphia Federation of Teachers, which was precisely what I wanted to do. And Philadelphia was a wonderful place, not only to live but also to work in labor union relations. And I would probably still be there today if I didn't care about coming back to Worcester for family and just to be here.

The law profession is not equalized between men and women and that's also one of the reasons why I'm in my own business. I own a law firm. Men still dominate the legal profession, within larger firms. It's very different working in an environment where you're expected to work 70 hours a week. It's what the expectations are, and especially if you're a new lawyer, you're expected to just be there as long as necessary, sometimes 11 o'clock at night. If the client's needs demand it, you just had to do the work. So when I went into my own practice, it was easier to make my own decisions about where I wanted to be when. My husband became very ill, so I was taking care of him, taking care of the children, and running my own law practice. So there was a lot of rebalancing. You always feel like wherever I am, I should be in two other places.

I think every experience you have enriches you, whether it's good or bad. If it's bad, you don't do it again. I'm very much an optimist, so I don't dwell on regret. I try to make the best of whatever circumstances I find myself in. Becoming a partner in a large law firm was never my idea of success. My idea of success in living is to have relationships with people which are meaningful. To feel that I'm helping people achieve something or be more comfortable or secure—whatever it is that I can do for them. And family relationships are a priority. I think you have to constantly review what path you're on and then take steps to see where it is you really want to go, not someone else's idea.

I think women are not equal in the workplace and I think that this generation of women will be disappointed because they think it is, and it really isn't. It happens that my profession is one where women do not predominate, even though they're graduating from law schools now at a higher percentage. But over the course of their career, they're not leading the profession. It's not that they're not talented. But it is a balancing act. You have to make your decisions between you and your partner, if you have one, how do we want to live? No one can tell you what it should be. I think the women that are out there now, the young women, are doing just wonderful things. And they're going to continue to do it, and they have freedoms that are just absolutely incredible.

Gale Nigrosh
Age 59
Interviewed on November 23, 2006 by Dan Long of Worcester State University

I came to Worcester in 1967. I had just been married to my first husband to whom I was married for 20 years. I was a student at Clark University, having left Barnard [College] at the end of my junior year. Barnard was one of the Seven Sisters colleges and there was, at the time that I was there, a regulation on the books called senior year in absentia. It was so common for women to be married at the end of their junior year, that they allowed you to do your senior year elsewhere and still graduate from Barnard. So I came to Clark, did my senior year, and I was invited to do a Master's at the same time. So I did two degrees simultaneously. I have a Master's of Arts in Teaching from Clark and I have a Doctorate in Linguistics from Brown.

I remember going to the bank to obtain a mortgage with my first husband in 1969. The only way that a woman could qualify on a mortgage was as a nurse or a teacher. Otherwise, nothing. And the mortgage was written in the husband's name and Et. Ux., meaning "and wife." So, I had no name even.

I faced a challenge at Clark when I was the youngest on the faculty in Romance Languages. It was traditional at that point in time that the newest got the most freshmen load. And I have to say, I fell in love with that level. I think that's what propelled me into the study of Linguistics because it was basic language acquisition that fascinated me. The field I pursued was Socio-Linguistics, which was very new at the time that I received my Doctorate in 1985.

What was frustrating to me was that there was no department of Linguistics at Clark. I really had to form my own network there of psychologists, sociologists, and English. This was interesting, but I was really ready to make a change when I did. I'm still connected with all my colleagues, and I've made new ones.

My first real job was at the Smithsonian Institution during the summer. It was a fabulous job. And then, of course, I was at school and I was in Barnard's babysitting program. And then I came to Worcester and my first job at

Clark was as an instructor. I think I got $6,000 a year at that time. I've always taught in one capacity or another. And I've done a lot of volunteer work; reading for children, reading with children. I remember my father always pointed out to me his cousin, Esther. And he would say to me, "Cousin Esther is a teacher." And she was so revered by the whole family. And then there were years when I wish that I was some successful business person. It was almost embarrassing to say I was a teacher because it's held in such low esteem in many places. But I intend to change that.

I now work with the Worcester Public Schools, creating partnerships with colleges and universities. Given that role, I have the privilege of being outside with people in the different colleges and universities. They're doing interesting things. I think one of the challenges and one of the successes has been building an awareness of a K [kindergarten] to 16 continuum, not a K to 12 and higher ed. And the people in K to 12 are the future clients of the people in the college and university system, and each needs to know how to cross the boundary into the other culture. I've seen so many connections made—faculty to faculty, student to student. It's been very exciting to see that starting to happen.

We have a program that started after the Education Reform Law was enacted in 1993. High school juniors and seniors can take college courses and get credit for high school courses, and sometimes they can get college credit. And now the money has dried up, but colleges in Worcester have generously kept the tradition alive so that students from the Worcester Public Schools can take courses at Assumption and Worcester State. We have students studying at Quinsigamond Community College and at Clark University. They're getting both college and high school credit. The College of the Holy Cross has a gifted high school student program. It's a year-long program. If a student is accepted, he or she can take a course each semester for credit.

I feel there are so many benefits from what I do. Mostly, that would involve the people and the feeling that I'm learning from them and I hope they're learning from me. I hope I'm making opportunities available.

I've been involved with the YWCA [Young Women's Christian Association], Daybreak [shelter for battered women], and Abby's House [shelter for battered women]. For a while I was involved with the Romanian Children's Relief. I wish I could do more but it's not always possible. I was a trustee at Temple Sinai where I'm a member. I was also on the Board of Directors of Dynamy [Experiential Educational Program]. All these organizations are quite different, but I'm interested in organizations that support women. I would say that what interests me most are programs for young women to really let them see what the possibilities are. I'm very, very committed to see more women and minorities get involved in engineering, math, and sciences. My own daughter was a Computer Science major at Carnegie Melon [University] And I'm committed to seeing people do what they love.

During the 1960s I was probably on every political march and demonstration. I was constantly in Washington protesting this and that. At this point, I no longer think that I can change the world. I've concentrated more on one person at a time, and I hope that I can make a difference.

Kay Bassett
Interviewed on October 23, 2007
by Elizabeth Irwin of the College
of the Holy Cross

I grew up in the Detroit area, in an automobile family. I

went to Ohio Wesleyan and was a Government/Political Science major. I met my husband there, although we didn't get married right away. I moved to Washington and worked for the Brookings Institute, a research organization, for just one year and then got married.

We went back to Ohio where my husband got a Master's Degree in English. I worked as a secretary part of the time, then I took over a few government classes from an older professor. We moved to Rochester, NY, and my husband received his Ph.D. [Doctor of Philosophy] from the University of Rochester. I was a retail buyer. I had my first child there.

Then we moved to Detroit, back to my roots, and my husband worked at Wayne State [University] and I had another child. So I was raising two children and working as a full- time wife and mother. I went back to school and got my MBA [Master's in Business Administration]. I worked in Detroit for Data General which was headquartered here in Westborough. We moved to North Carolina. Data General transferred me to their Research and Development Lab, so I actually have a high tech background with my MBA. My career really was in technical management. I worked in that for 17 years.

We moved from North Carolina to Cleveland where my husband became Dean of Arts and Sciences at Case Western Reserve. I went to work for NASA [National Aeronautics and Space Administration] as a contractor, managing their desktop services. The work I did at NASA was challenging and it was great. It was a research environment, so it was a little like a university. I was almost like a CIO [Chief Information Officer]. However, when you do contracting with the government, there is a counterpart who is actually a civil servant. I wasn't a civil servant, but I had to implement the ideas with my counterpart and all of the information technology on my NASA site.

We moved to Worcester in 2000 when my husband became President of Clark University. And in another career change, I became the wife of the President. I had a lot of contacts in this area from my Data General days. I had the option of going back to work or being more active in the community and on campus. I decided to take advantage of being on campus.

When I was growing up, there was no question that I would go to college. Back then a woman normally went to college to become a teacher, nurse, or wife. But I happened to be in school in the 1960s and that was a transforming period. And women started talking about more options. I was privileged in a way because my father always treated me with a certain amount of achievement expectation. My mother did, too, but I think my father understood it more. He was extremely proud when I earned my MBA, and my husband has been incredibly supportive. My husband's schedule was a bit more flexible than mine so we were able to balance that career-family thing. Also, I was in an area with IT [Information Technology] and business where I was able to move with him, and still find opportunities within my career.

Carrie Johnson
Age 58
Interviewed by Maureen Ryan Doyle and Charlene L. Martin on March 25, 2011 at Assumption College

So I was able to go to college in California. I majored in Journalism and really didn't know what I wanted to do, but somebody said that I was a good writer, so I started writing for the newspaper. And in college I worked as a public relations person for the Community Youth Gang Services Project. Back then there were a lot of innocent people dying from gangs. It was an awakening to me. All of a sudden I was put in the middle of all this. When somebody got killed or we had to talk to gang members, here I am talking to these guys and trying to figure out where they're coming from and where they're going, getting them on television programs, getting people to know them, and do public service announcements. And it was a challenge, but I guess I was young enough to jump in and idealistic enough to fit in, and make a difference.

I was there [in that job] for about two years before I moved back to Massachusetts. I wanted to come home. I went to work for the *Metro West Daily News* as their first black reporter. When I came back to Framingham, there were so many more black faces. Some things had changed, change for the better as far as I was concerned. Here I am their first black reporter, and they were walking around on eggshells at first, tripping over themselves…trying not to offend or say the wrong thing. I feel I'm good at bringing people around, being a reasonable person. Eventually it all came around and we all worked well together. I made some good friendships and I enjoyed it. I went from there to the *Telegram & Gazette*.

I ended up leaving there [the *Telegram & Gazette*] because I started a cleaning company. I actually started it to make some extra money, and I started making more money there than I did at the *Telegram & Gazette*. It grew to be a three and one-half million dollar company, and I had 165 employees. I started the business with my sister and a girlfriend, but after a couple of years they left. I did get another partner five years in…It probably could have gotten a lot bigger had we really known what we were doing, watched the industry like you're supposed to. I'm very good at teaching business planning now. And I use my company, Sparkle Cleaning, as a case study.

We were women in a male-dominated industry. Women clean well, but men are masters at making money at it. And then here we come, trying to call ourselves competitors. So, we ran into that a lot where the first time we walked into a conference room with 12 guys in business suits, and there's us, 12 white men in business suits and…everybody's jaws would kind of drop to the ground, including ours. It was tough getting into corporate America because they weren't kicking the doors open for us. So, we got involved in the 8A Program, which is a program to help minority businesses compete in getting government contracts. We worked with the SBA [Small Business Administration] and ended up doing quite well. We did Hanscom [Air Force Base], we did [Fort] Devens, we did Newport for the Navy. We did federal buildings in Maine. And we did a lot of post offices. We were in four states: Maine, New Hampshire, Rhode Island, and Massachusetts.

Seventeen years [later] we sold it. Sparkle is still going on. It helped me grow as a person, it helped me feel like I was worth something. I sent two kids to college, bought a house, got rid of my Flintstone car and bought a real car, and took my kids on vacation. I wrote a book about my experience and it's called *From the Pits to the Palace*.

I started teaching at the CWE [Center for Work and Enterprise] a long time ago, and I just love it. I do a 14-week Business Planning course. And then I said that I wanted to try college, and I'm at Quinsigamond [Community College]. They started me out with Business Ethics, and it's a great time to teach Business Ethics with all the material that's out there. And now this semester I'm teaching Speech Communications.

There's two quotes that are all about everything that I value, that I try to convey in talking to women, because we just need it. One is, Confucius say, "The greatest glory is not in never falling, but in rising every time you fall." And the other is…we'll go from Confucius to Henry Ford. "Whether you think you can or you think you can't, you're right."

Mercy Akpan
Interviewed on November 11, 2005 by Brooke Correa of Worcester State University

I was born in Nigeria, West Africa. I came to the United States to go to school, and I ended up settling here. I went to Central State University in Oklahoma and I went to Oklahoma City University for my MBA [Master's in Business Administration], concentrating in Marketing and Promotions. I came to Worcester because my husband relocated here in search of a job.

I have worked as long as I can remember, but the work I am doing right now is what I enjoy the most. I have been ministering to people in need for three years. I believe that God created me for this work. He stirred me into finding purpose for my life. He created me for this and I feel really fulfilled. I work with families, the homeless, and battered women.

My goal is to leave an imprint or legacy that will help alleviate human sufferings. My goal is to embrace these people with the love of God, and let them know they are important, and to spread the good news of the gospel of Jesus Christ. I try to link people in need to where they can get help. I reach out to the young, the orphans, and to offer homes to the homeless. I also distribute things like vitamins, food, and clothing. We have a program where we visit the sick in hospitals, supply food to the needy, supply clothing, offer prayers, counseling, and even provide transportation to those who are unable to provide for themselves.

I think that people are skeptical to come to God at first. But if you don't shove this down their throats, if you reach out to them in love, they come to understand. There are so many churches around, but still there are people who are not responding. They would rather go shopping than go to a prayer group or a support group. But that will change, that is changing.

We should pray for our city and for the government who is in power, so they will come to know the God Almighty who created Worcester in the first place. God put them in office to take care of the poor, the homeless, the addicts, and the children.

Worcester has opened my eyes and my heart to understand human suffering. I have become more sensitive and attentive to the needs of people. Knowing that God is here for me gets me through the rough times. His presence is everything to me. Once you have the peace of God, the joy of the Lord is in you, and that's what gets me through.

Rosemary Marshall
Age 52
Interviewed on April 11, 2008 by Nicole Jimino and Brian Zarthar from Assumption College

I was born in Worcester, grew up in Shrewsbury, but I live in Worcester now. After high school, I went to the Manning School of Commercial Art and then to the Art Institute of Boston. I loved it, but I knew that if I wanted to really pursue a career in art, I would have to move out of Worcester. I did not want to move out of Worcester. My now-husband and I were planning to get married. He already had a job in Worcester, and I was not willing to relocate.

I worked at Digital Equipment as a technical illustrator. After my first child was born, I was a stay-at-home-mom. I also ran an art business, which I still run. I do watercolors and calligraphy and house portraits. I also work for Sodexho Food Services at Charlie's at Assumption

College. My schedule here at Charlie's and the art business are perfectly balanced. We use the school schedule and I have a big semester break and a long break in the summer. Calligraphy is big in the summertime with graduations and weddings. I'm really busy right before Christmas with painting. A lot of people call me to do house portraits that time of year.

I have six children. When my youngest went to school, I was lonely. I still wanted to be a stay-at-home-mom, but I wanted to be around people. I've always liked cooking, and I like the pace of food service. So I just got involved with this, and the schedule works out perfectly.

I'm really happy that I have found this really great balance. I feel fortunate because not everybody can do that. I'm not the main breadwinner. That's another privilege I have. I don't have that pressure. My husband runs a successful business and he's the main breadwinner. You have to make a choice and I'm happy to be able to make this choice.

I've been involved with Little League for the past 25 years. I run the snack shack, I coach a Little League team, I'm on the all-star coaching staff. If we keep winning, that goes right through August. We host a lot of tournaments: the High School State Tournaments, Little League Division State Tournament, Senior Division for 13 to 16 year-olds, and the East Region Tournament. It keeps us hopping, but it's fun, and I love it. I have a real passion for this.

When I was growing up, it was a more chauvinistic society. Men were considered more important, and even women considered men more important. The women's movement came along and opened people's eyes. We realized that we are all in this together. I have been blessed with so many things. I have to be thankful every day. I'm happy that I stayed at home with my kids.

Ivana Pellegrino
Age 48
Interviewed on November 2, 2005 by Stephanie Dudek of Worcester State University

I was born in Italy in a little town called Calabria that looked very medieval. It was very beautiful. I was very little when I left Italy and so much is different now.

My mother's sister was here and she had just lost her husband. So my mother felt that since my aunt was all by herself with her kids, she would come here to help. I have three sisters and three brothers. I am the baby girl.

My father was a carpenter in Italy. When we came to this country, my father really didn't speak English. So one of my father's cousins took him to a construction company, Amorello Construction, and he worked there for almost 30 years. My mother worked at Dino's Restaurant. She later opened a pizza place. And then at the age of 64 she opened up Palma's Bakery. And that's how I became a baker.

I have worked at many jobs. I worked at Worcester Molded Plastic, at Come Play [Products Company], and I worked at hairdressing. I have a license for that. And I worked at a nursing home, Saint Vincent Home. The elderly make you laugh. I would go there in a bad mood, and they would make me laugh. Everyone knew my name, and I used to even take them home. I used to take them out on weekends, out to eat, I used to take them everywhere. I loved them. That was my favorite job. I would do that again! I love working with people, helping people. Sometimes I get frustrated because people don't understand…you're tired and people demand things. You're not working for yourself, you're working for them, for the public. But when you work for the elderly, it's so much fun.

Worcester gave me a lot of opportunity, a lot of business opportunity. When we first came here, people didn't even know what espresso was. And so it really gave us an opportunity to open something Italian, and I know people love Italian people and love Italian food. Not everybody goes to another country and becomes successful. I wouldn't call it luck, it's just hard work. When I'm not home, I'm at work. I work six to six, seven days a week. I work hard and there's not enough time to do anything.

If I ever win Mass Millions [lottery], there's one thing I would do. I would house the homeless. When you don't have nothing, and you don't have a house or food, it's terrible. Some people say, "Go to work." But when people go through so much and try to get a job, it's sad. You see more and more homeless because things are so high, people can't afford it. How can anyone afford first, last, and deposit? If I ever win the million, I wouldn't give it to any charity. I would go and see which family is poor, and I would hand it to them directly.

I moved back to Italy for a while. I married there and opened my own business, hairdressing. My husband had his own business, selling cars, but he sold it because I was sad all the time. All my family was here, and I missed them. So we moved back here and my husband works at Amorello Construction. My husband and I have been married for 20 years. I have a daughter, Gilda who is 19. She was born in Italy. I have a son, Roberto, who was born in the United States.

Women should be respected and seen in a good way. Hopefully when we go up to heaven, if there is one, I think that we should have a special place. We do a lot. We go through the pain. Sometimes men will help you out, like my husband will help clean and cook, but it's not like the girl. The girl is special. I'm not against men, but we go through a lot of pain. We know how to handle pain, so we should be looked at as something special.

I love this country to death, but there are a lot of wrong things. And that is why this country is high on everything—on drugs, on divorce, on kids running away from home. There is no more sitting down at the table with the whole family at once. It's chaotic. We are rushing trying to get too much money. What is money when you can have a family?

Gail England
Age 48
Interviewed on April 18, 2006 by Monique England, her daughter, of Worcester State University

I come from an intact family. My mother and father had four children and I'm the oldest. My mother was a stay-at-home mother. My father worked 70 hours a week to support the family. He was a businessman who owned his own business for 50 years. He owned a service station. After my siblings and I grew up and left home, my mother worked part-time for my father. And she did all the housework.

My mother did a very good job raising me. It was different back then. You didn't have the conveniences of jumping in a car. It was one car per family. So you basically stayed in your neighborhood. You went to your neighborhood school. All your friends were neighborhood children. Nowadays you are a taxicab service. I was bringing my children from friends to friends, from town to town.

I started teaching dancing in 1982. I was out of high school and just got married. I used to dance myself, five or six classes a week. Then this opportunity came along and I taught dancing for nine years.

My immediate friends did not attend college. They eventually went to college, but not right away. They all worked. One girl became a CPA [Certified Public Accountant], but other than that we all went to work, and after a few years decided what to do. Some of us got married, I believe all of us got married. Some of us divorced. Some of us had children, some of us have no children.

I have three children, one girl and two boys. I have stayed home with the children, and I have worked with the children. It's very difficult to achieve that balance of children and work. You need to spread yourself out. You can't be perfect either.

I enjoyed staying home. When I had my third child, I stayed home for a few years. Then I knew it was time to work full-time. The kids were getting older, they were going to high school, and there were a lot of financial necessities.

A typical day for me starts at four in the morning with half a pot of coffee and a newspaper. I make sure I read the news and every day I watch the news. I know what's going on in the world. I make lunches, if needed, for a couple of the kids. I drive my son to the bus stop at 6:30 every morning. I come back, get myself going, pick up the house a bit, and head to work at 8:00.

I work at the Worcester Juvenile Court on Highland Street. I've worked there for seven years. I previously worked for the Worcester Superior Court from 1976, the year I graduated, to 1985, the year I had my first child. Fourteen months later I had my second child and four and a half years later, I had my third child.

I went back to work for financial reasons. We had previously bought a two-family house. And we thought the second income would supplement, so I wouldn't have to go back to work right away. And it did. And my husband took on a second job. It worked for a while, quite a few years. I worked dancing a little bit part-time and I also worked for the family business part-time. I worked about 12 to 14 hours a week. I worked at night.

I now work in the Probation Department. I do data entry along with helping people, helping attorneys, helping DYS [Department of Youth Services], helping DSS [Department of Social Services]. And we have a busy day. It is difficult working full- time now because I still have three children and we have to juggle the schedule. We have basketball and we have soccer. There are lessons. Fortunately, I have a job where I am able to use my comp [compensation] time, run out for an hour, and come back. I use my comp time all the time. With three children you have the responsibility of getting to and from doctor's appointments and other kinds of appointments. It's a busy day.

I found this job online and called up. I believe they hired me because they saw that I had worked for the other court for ten years. I had an interview and was hired the next day. Going into the workforce was very difficult. I was close to 40 years old, trying to get a full-time job and my computer skills were not there. I took a computer course at WPI [Worcester Polytechnic Institute], one of the night courses. It was difficult because I wasn't very familiar with the computer, all those programs like Microsoft and Excel. You just had to learn it.

I have a really nice boss and she's just a few years older than I. We get along fine. There are five of us left in our department. Because of the state's financial matters, they have been laying people off. My boss is a female and she worked her way from a probation officer to an assistant chief. She was made a chief probation officer for Worcester County. That includes four courts: Worcester, Milford, Fitchburg, and Dudley, and part-time for Leominster.

It's 2006. Gas prices are over three dollars a gallon. Tuition for a state college is thousands of dollars. If I weren't working now, I would go under. I was a stay-at-home mother at one point. I ran functions, a flea market at one point. I made hot dogs, I made pancakes, I sold teddy bears and popcorn. I did these things because I found time to be involved in the school. I think I've done pretty well for myself. I've raised three good kids.

I consider the primary work of my life to be my family. I have to do the housework, the wash, many kinds of things that come around the house. My job is secondary, but

I need it to survive 2006. It's very difficult. My husband works for the city and I work for the state. There are benefits working for the state. I get a decent amount of vacation time and sick time. I can use my sick time for my kids and our family, which is very good. And I get comp time. I get personal time. I get insurance, if I need it. My husband works for the city and gets the same kind of package.

There is much work that needs to be done at home. I am the last one to leave in the morning and when I come back, I need to come home and start cooking, get homework done, get things done. There's a lot of work to do. When I come home from my work job at 4:30, I come home to my second job…my house job. And that lasts until about 11:00 at night. I have to get everything done and then it starts all over again. So, basically I work 20 hours a day and it never ends.

Jean Laquidara Hill
Age 46
Interviewed on November 19, 2006 by Hayley Stefan of Worcester State University

I have lived in East Boston, in an Italian neighborhood, a completely Italian neighborhood. Then in Wilmington, Massachusetts, an Italian neighborhood. Then Boston. When I got married, we moved to Westboro for three years and then Oxford. When my husband and I got married, it was the first time I was in a neighborhood that wasn't Italian. I mean nobody came over and dipped their bread in your sauces or ate your meatballs. It was different.

My father was very warm, very, very hard-working. He worked in the garment industry until he was 46. He was the manager, and the industry up and left Massachusetts. He put a mortgage on our house and went and bought a little grocery store. And we all worked there. My mother was very strong, very hard-working. She stayed home to take care of us. Later she got a job as a housekeeper because that allowed her ultimate freedom of hours, and to be her own boss.

I did my Bachelor's at Northeastern University. And I did some of my Master studies at Northeastern, at Emerson, and at Harvard. I did the five-year co-op [cooperative] program at Northeastern. I have a B.S. [Bachelor of Science] in Science Education, High School Science Ed. I faced some challenges as a college student. I had no money. And no one in my family had ever gone to college. And while they were very supportive of learning, my family thought it was very progressive of them to not financially support me, but to give me the old pat on the back. They thought I could go to school for a couple of years to have some job to fall back on, so when I got married, I would have something in case my husband died. There were times when my family, as wonderful as they are, kind of saw me as a slacker because other members of the family stayed and worked at my father's store.

And I went off to college. I worked full-time. That was very, very hard. But I was young and I had energy and I saw it as such an incredible opportunity that I must say, I just loved it.

I work at the Worcester *Telegram & Gazette* now. After college I was a high school science teacher. I took a job working a little bit at a paper and was asked to do a column a week. I said sure, and I got addicted, absolutely addicted. And from there I waited for an opening on the *Telegram & Gazette*, just for the stringer's job. I worked hard at that. And then basically when I went full-time, it was a checkbook issue. There wasn't enough money in our checkbook to keep up with the bills of having three children and saving for college. The youngest was three, and I thought I could juggle a job around their hours and my responsibilities. And that's what I did. After being a stringer for the *Telegram & Gazette* for eight years, I interviewed for a full-time job. And I got it.

I have five children and my youngest two are in college. But it's pretty scary at times, doing all of it, juggling. Let's just say that in one of my worst nightmares I'd wake up in the middle of the night and think that I missed one of my children's important soccer games. And it's just the worst feeling. I'd be so wrapped up in work and my own thoughts and my own responsibilities, separate from the family. I was always worried about missing something very important to my family. Sometimes I felt like I didn't have the emotional direction or elasticity, sometimes I just felt like I was too tired to care enough about every little thing that was going on. My husband is incredible, he's a super dad. He thoroughly enjoys all our children, and always did. The part that would press on me more was that the schedule seemed to be my responsibility.

I'm happy. I think I'm in the field that I belong in. If somebody had told me when I was 22 that I was going to be a reporter and not a high school science teacher, I would have thought they were drinking a lot of something. For me the most meaningful part of being a reporter is to go out there and find a story that I think somebody else might want to know about. And it gives me the chance to tell that story, to tell somebody else's story.

I covered a story for the paper that changed my life. Many churches in Worcester County were sending individuals to help the people of Haiti. It was an overwhelming commitment from Protestant and Catholic churches. I went there and covered it first-hand so that others back in Worcester would understand why the churches and volunteers were so committed. The people there are so poor. Most of them have one meal a day. If the churches weren't helping, no children would be eating. I think it helped me to see the good that organized religion can do. So no children would be eating, no children would be educated, and there would be no opportunity for them to ever support themselves. And that's all done by organized religion.

I used my vacation time to go to Haiti and wrote about it when I returned home. And it was something I really, really fought for. I fought to spend my own money and my own time. I met a16 year-old, who belonged to a Baptist church, who was committed to going over there and spending her April vacation there. I thought what could be so compelling that this 16 year-old would want to go and live in pretty difficult conditions? I guess you could say that she led me there. I had to go there. I almost adopted a baby from there, but she was very ill and died before the whole process was completed. But I think I was meant to go there and I think I was meant to tell the stories. We ran a series in the paper and I can only hope that somebody ended up doing something meaningful for someone in Haiti.

I don't think that there's anything you can't do. You need some time just being with yourself, and dream, and say to yourself, "What would I do if I could do anything?" And try to do that. We only get to live once. Follow your heart as much as your head.

Rev. Jill Williams
Age 27
Interviewed on November 23, 2008 by Ali Marinelli and Zachary DeLoughery of Assumption College

I have a Bachelor of Arts in English Literature and Theatre Performance. I also have a Master's in Divinity from Virginia

Theological Seminary. I took a year off between college and getting my Master's Degree. You quickly find out that a Bachelor's Degree doesn't mean as much as it used to.

At one point I was going to marry a man who was going to be a minister. I was going to be a minister's wife and work in Christian Education. But my call just changed and I sensed that God was calling me. It is not a usual thing for a woman to be a priest. I felt very much that there needed to be a younger female voice in the priesthood, saying that it doesn't always have to be older men who are relating to God. Women can relate to that instantly as well, that God speaks to all of God's children, male and female, and so having someone specifically to represent them…that became important to me.

In the Episcopal Church you go through a year-long discernment process. That involves meeting with several committees and people to discuss your sense of call and where it comes from. If you get through that process, and many people agree that you are called to ministry, you pursue a Master's Degree. When you finish school, you look for a job. I now work at St. Francis Church in Holden. St. Francis is my home parish, so I didn't think that I would be coming home. Jesus wasn't accepted in his hometown, so I didn't think that I would be coming home to Massachusetts. I thought I would be someplace in the South. But the rector there reached out and said, "You know, we want a younger female type." I'm the first female priest St. Francis has had.

I love what I do. I get to preach the gospel, and hopefully, reach a different group of people. I work closely with pastoral care, and specifically pastoral care for women. Since the Episcopal Church has a very liturgical tradition, I dress in an alb and stole for church. They don't even make priests' clothes very well for women yet. And there are all these little girls in my congregation who have probably never seen a woman dressed like that, standing up and presiding at the element, and preaching a sermon…a sermon that I hope is relatively balanced between being emotional, educational, theological, and intellectual. I never saw that growing up, and now they can.

CHAPTER FOUR

HEALTH

"…. we do ask for women equal medical advantages with those enjoyed by men."

> Harriet K. Hunt, physician
> Proceedings, October 24, 1850, morning session of the First National Woman's Rights Convention

In early 19th century America, women faced a variety of health challenges due to their gender. Women were not allowed to attend medical school and so there were no female physicians, the demands of old-world dressing codes restricted their bodies, little attention was paid to women's health issues in research and in practice, and they were quick to be diagnosed as mentally ill. It is no wonder that the attendees of the First National Woman's Rights Convention demanded that more attention be paid to the health needs of women.

Fashion may seem to be a frivolous topic, but corsets not only limited movement, they often injured internal organs. Dress reform movements developed in America and Europe and one of the arguments questioned the sacrifice of health over fashionable dress prescribed by social norms.

Even more distressing was the lack of female physicians. One of the reasons that Elizabeth Blackwell wanted to go into medicine was that she knew many women found it difficult to discuss their health concerns with male doctors. She was turned down by every medical school until she was finally accepted by Geneva Medical College in New York. It is said that the college asked the male students to vote on the acceptance of women and, thinking it was a joke, they voted to approve. Elizabeth became the first female medical student and faced the shock, anger, and prejudice of the male students and faculty. Some wanted her to absent herself from certain "delicate" lectures, but she would not. In 1849, Blackwell became the first woman to achieve a medical degree in the United States. Since she was then banned from practice in most hospitals, she went to Paris but had to continue her training as a student midwife, not a physician. Barriers to studying and practicing medicine remained in place for many years.

What Dr. Blackwell and other women of that time knew was that women's health was at risk with treatment by only male doctors. Aside from the modesty of women that made them hesitate to seek advice from male doctors, it was the doctors themselves who were restricted from treating their female patients appropriately. They were not allowed to view women's naked bodies and so examined them through their clothes and even avoided looking during childbirth. Medical students learned about women's bodies from textbooks and mannequins.

Beyond the issues of modesty, the medical field viewed women differently in other ways. Since discussing anything of a sexual nature was unthinkable between female patient and male doctor, women lacked information about birth control and sexually transmitted diseases. The natural female passages from puberty through menopause were often treated as a disease. Mental illness was often blamed on menstruation, pregnancy, and menopause. Any verbal outbursts or forceful demands by 19th century women were likely to result in their being labeled "hysterical." The recommended cure for such hysteria was bed rest, isolation, and no intellectual activities. If the treatment sounds harmless, one need only read Charlotte Perkins Gilman's 1892 short story *The Yellow Wallpaper*. Her tale depicts a woman suffering from post-partum depression who eventually succumbs to madness while undergoing such treatment. It highlights the physical and mental health issues for women of that time.

Today women may choose female or male doctors, have access to information about preventive healthcare, and more medical research is being conducted using women subjects. Medical careers are no longer limited to nurse or midwife. Yet the stories in this chapter reveal continuing concern about issues that affect women's physical, mental, and emotional health. Some of these issues include coping with a disease while others involve sexual abuse, eating disorders, or addictions. Many of the women share stories of being caregivers, a role still assumed by more females than males in the United States. They care for husbands, children, and aging relatives often while also working full-time.

Those who choose a healthcare profession certainly demonstrate that our society has moved way beyond restricting women from practicing medicine. Some of these women have stories of deciding to be a nurse when that was the only healthcare role available to them at the time while others tell of becoming doctors, therapists, and EMTs [Emergency Medical Technicians]. All mention the balance they must find between the demands of a stressful career and their roles as wife and mother.

It is easy to take for granted the privileges we have today and the struggles of those who went before us. While substantial barriers have broken down due to the courageous women who confronted the status quo, we are also reminded that even today women face unique health challenges. This chapter focuses on the ways women negotiate their physical and emotional well-being both in their personal and family lives and in relation to the public institutions that make up our healthcare system. We learn about how women view, care for, and project their bodies and minds introspectively and in relation to the outside world.

Mary Aleksiewicz
Age 59
Interviewed on October 26, 2005
by Danielle Deyoria
of Worcester State University

You want to say the pat answer, "I wanted to help people," but I have always been told that I am a very optimistic person, and I think that it was in my nature to be in the service profession. At the time, we were limited: a teacher, a nurse, or a secretary. And teaching wasn't really an interest of mine, and being the oldest in the family it had always been left to me to take care of the other children or if anyone got sick, the responsibility was put on me. So I think a lot of that geared me to want to help others. It was the way I was brought up, in a way. My father was very much against my becoming a nurse because his image of nursing at that time was bedpans. I had my heart set on Mass General [Hospital]. So, he went down to Mass General with me for an interview with the Guidance Counselor. He came out of there thinking it was the best thing since sliced white bread. She was able to show him it wasn't just emptying bedpans. As a matter of fact, he became the biggest advocate of nursing after that. He fell in love with Mass General and fell in love with the field of nursing. And remained one of its biggest supporters until the day he died.

We need more faculty. We have waiting lists now, I know at Quinsigamond [Community College] I have met with students that said there is about a three to four year waiting list to get into the [Nursing] program. They are accepted but they have to wait three years before they can begin. And the reason for that is the shortage of faculty. So we did a good job in getting people interested into nursing and coming into the field of nursing, we raised the wages; there are just so many options now. People see it as a whole different profession now, more than just bedside nursing and bedpan nursing just as my father did.

My love and greatest achievement is family. As far as the hospital, I think [my] greatest achievement is as a clinician. I know that I have affected a lot of lives, even when I did chemo [chemotherapy], ICU [Intensive Care Unit], ER [Emergency Room]—you are talking to an old-time nurse. I have done it all and to really know that I have made a difference—to get letters from patients, families writing to you that you made a difference is just a wonderful feeling to be able to do something like that. As an administrator [Vice President of Nursing], it is known that I can make this hospital a better work environment for the nurses and also that I can basically coordinate and plan nursing care and nursing practice to provide the best for patients here at Fairlawn [Rehabilitation Hospital].

Worcester has grown tremendously as a city. In terms that we now have UMass [University of Massachusetts Memorial Hospital and Medical School] which I remember when all that was open was the basement. I worked at St. V's [Saint Vincent Hospital] because that was a large hospital. There is Memorial [Hospital]; a lot of the small hospitals closed. I have always worked at large teaching hospitals and when I came here, I had no intention of staying. It was just close to where my children were going to school and I could get to them. I started out per diem. However, you know I just loved what I was doing and I had a lot of opportunities to do a lot of different things. I loved it. I think that Worcester has gained a lot in terms of medical opportunities. We now have St. V's; Memorial and UMass have joined together. The community hospitals have closed. Now we have specialties like acute rehab which we never had in Central Mass before 1987.

We have three women on the Senior Management Team—you would not have seen that years ago. We have had a female CEO [Chief Executive Officer] here, a lot of the HealthSouth facilities, one, two, three, four out of— sorry, five out of seven are women CEO's in the New England area. I am seeing more women in the leadership positions. I am seeing more women in higher paying jobs. I am seeing more women being more respected for what they do.

The Nurse Association, the Nurse Executives that I belong to, used to be just nurse managers with a separate group for nursing. Now it is just one group, and it has truly found a voice. We are looking at healthcare issues and have become a strong voice because of the unity. It is for good, solid reasons; good causes we are fighting for … and I think that is what is different. We are an organization and we have found a voice and we are being heard.

Joanne Wilcox
Age 24
Interviewed on October 26, 2005 by Melanie Wilcox of Worcester State University

I took the EMT [Emergency Medical Technician] course during my junior year of college, not for credit, but just for something to do. I did that as a job my senior year and I loved [it] and just kind of continued on with it after school. I took the Paramedic program two years ago now I'd say, and finished up last December.

You meet all kinds of people. Different stories, different problems, different ways of life—you learn something new every time you meet people. I like helping people, I like helping them feel better, I like knowing that I'm making a difference in somebody's world.

It's tough [as a female] if you let people get to you because a lot of the older generation people will—they're not used to seeing, basically, females in uniform. So, you'll go up to their house—I get it at least once every day—"You're such a little thing, how are you gonna help me?" Yeah, I'm small, but that doesn't hold me back at all. Usually I'm the only female on the scene—all my partners are male and all the firemen that show up are male. [It's] not unusual [for a paramedic to be female], it's just a male-dominated field and people just aren't used to seeing women in roles like that I guess.

If you listen to a lunchtime conversation, say, among paramedics, you'd probably be kind of disturbed because we'll....joke about stuff that really isn't funny. But you have to have a sense of humor about it because if you let every call get to you and get under your skin, you won't be able to perform the job. I mean every once in a while, something affects you.

Just last night I went to a call. It had come in as a kid saying his babysitter wouldn't wake up. So, we got there and both the kids are in diapers—one of the kids is like a year and a half and the other can't be older than three—in the house, woman's down on the floor. She was drunk out of her mind. But that—I mean that bothered me. We took her to the hospital and the cops stayed at the house so somebody would watch the kids 'til they got hold of the parents. They're probably going to have to file a 51A [Section 51A of the Massachusetts General Laws, reporting of suspected abuse or neglect] on her [babysitter] which is like child neglect. I mean you don't babysit kids drunk. That just bothers me. But anything to do with kids especially bothers me. They're helpless, you know.

Lynda Young, M.D.
Age 63
Interviewed on January 13, 2011 by Maureen Ryan Doyle and Charlene L. Martin

The day I turned 16 I started working as a nurse's aide at Kenmore Mercy Hospital in Kenmore, New York. I was an aide in physical therapy. My sister worked there also and she was a nurse's aide in the same department. My uncle was an obstetrician in Kenmore and was head of OB at that hospital—which is how I got the job frankly. And I worked right until the time I went to medical school. I was a nurse's aide. So it was great because I always had a job on weekends and I always had a job all summer because we used to fill in when other aides would take vacations. So I learned a variety of things with that. I learned: (a) I did not want to be a nurse's aide the rest of my life [laughs], (b) I thought I'd be a nurse, and then when I would go off to the floor to help out on the floor as an aide I thought, "I don't know about that." And I thought, "I like what *he* does." [Laughs] And it was always a "he" or most likely a "he." So that's when I kind of decided—and actually before that I was always going to be a teacher—I mean who wasn't in the '50s, '60s? So that's when I decided that I wanted to go into medical school. What's interesting is that my aunt and uncle, the obstetrician and the nurse, my godparents, told me that it was no job for a woman and that I should think about doing something else. [Laughs] Being me I probably said, "Really? Well, I'll show you." I maybe never said it out loud, but that was my attitude. My parents were very encouraging. And then afterwards my uncle was very, very encouraging once I got into medical school. He would take me to some of his medical meetings and that sort of thing.

I went to the State University of New York at Buffalo Medical School … I was lucky enough to get into Buffalo early decision so I knew in October of my senior year of college that I was going there. So that was very, very nice…. and, again tuition was a big factor, tuition was $800 a semester. That's because you were in-state and that made a big difference. There were 105—I had 105 classmates, six of us were women. And I distinctly remember the interview where I was told that they did not like to admit women because they just got married, had a family, and quit. And that's what I was told by the dean of the medical school. [That was in] 1969.

So there's a few more little things about medical school [laughs]. The thing I remember the best was Anatomy. All my partners were guys…I don't even know what we were studying, but it was in Anatomy lab so we were there with cadavers and it was a huge room and there were four students to a cadaver so there were 25 tables or something like that—it was a big room. And the head of the lab asked the women to leave so that the men could— whatever it was that we were going to discuss they didn't think it was appropriate for women to hear. And to this day [emphasizes], I am angry with myself that I left the room. And we stood outside the door and we started to rabble-rouse and we said, "Did you pay the same amount of tuition as they did in there?" And we all said, "Yes, yes." And,

"What are we doing out here?" "Oh, we don't want to make them angry because you know he gives us our grades and blah, blah, blah." So we stood there like good little girls. And then afterwards we went in and ran up to our partners and said, "What was this all about?" [Laughs]. And they said it was really ridiculous, it was probably scatological, they just didn't think that we should hear it. That's one thing that stands out in my mind. [Laughs].

To get involved in [my] community has been probably one of the best things that I've done and that I try to encourage people to do. And it's a time crunch and there's also the older physician whose entire life is consumed by medicine and the younger physicians who want a life outside of their profession. A lot of people say medicine is no longer a profession, it's a job, and I think that's true, I think that's true. I don't like to look at it that way though because I think it's a profession. The advice would be to kind of look at it more professional, not just think, "Oh, I have to go to work today, but I'll be done by five." Well, lucky you if you're done by five. That doesn't happen very often. [Laughs] But you have a unique place in your community.

In '96 to '97 I think it was, I was the first woman President of the Worcester District [Medical Society] in 220 years ...... And that was a good year; it was good to get involved. After a while I became a lot more involved with the [Massachusetts] Medical Society ... and people kept coming up to me saying, "You really ought to put your name in to do this, to do that." They said, "Put your name in for an officer." And I said, "Oh you know, okay fine."

It took me four years, but I finally get on the nomination for Vice-President. The way it goes is Vice-President, President-Elect, President. Vice-President to President-Elect isn't a done deal. You have to go before nominating again, but once you're president-elect you automatically move up. [So I am President-Elect of the

Massachusetts Medical Society and] it is such a great opportunity, such a great opportunity for me.

Tara Pandolfi
Age 31
Interviewed on November 17, 2006 by Maddie Gambale of Worcester State University

I work at Planned Parenthood League of Massachusetts. I'm a health education specialist. I do HIV [Human Immunodeficiency Virus] counseling and other types of counseling there. [This work has] meant a lot to me as a woman. And I just love the work that we do there, the service that we provide, and the people we provide it for. The effect that women's rights has for me.

I've done [community service] things through Planned Parenthood. Volunteer work, like shelters and schools. Doing presentations at schools that's not paid for. Presentations about sex education, about the importance of sexual health and stuff like that. I would do volunteer HIV testing [at the shelters]. You know, I would do volunteer passing out of condoms at shelters in the city of Worcester. I think that [Planned Parenthood] is good at getting the information out and distributed evenly among the populations. And that they're good advocates for women, providing services like that.

I just think that women have come a long way and our rights have come a long way. I think there's still a long way to go as far as equality. And also, I really feel that women's rights under the age of 18 should be really captured. They're not—they don't really have any rights.

I hope I would have a legacy, especially through the work I do at Planned Parenthood. I'm hoping that my help is my biggest effort and that people remember that and feel that. There's a lot of emotional issues there. So it can be—

there can be some very hard days. We're given a very emotional job.

Judith White
Age 47
Interviewed on April 7, 2008 by
Katelyn Ziter and
Meghan Ray
of Assumption College

It's actually not [a sensitive subject] for me because I had health issues that are so bizarre that—a lot of time it's something that no one ever knows about. I had what they call chiari malformation. It took my physician almost three years to diagnose it. And I talked to other people and it took them six years, eight years. And it's a brain malformation. Of course, I tease because I say it explains a lot [laughs].

It's a brain malformation and I had to go to Boston to have it corrected. The neurosurgeon in Worcester said, "Oh, I've done it a couple of times," and the neurosurgeon in Boston said, "I've done it a couple of times a week." Forty miles to the east is like night and day in the medical field.

So, a lot of people have had it and never knew they had it. Other than that I run, I work out, I skate with the boys, I have my own hockey skates because they all play hockey. We put a rink up in the backyard for the winter. We have a pool so I swim and cannonball and dive and do all that fun stuff in the summer. No [health issues] besides that little hiccup.

I think it made me realize—because my kids were young and here I am leaving my youngest—let's see my youngest was four—and here I am leaving to go to Boston for brain surgery. That's kind of scary. So, I think I look at life like, "Well, you only go around once." I'm not like a daredevil or anything like that. I'm gonna put my hockey skates on and I'm gonna skate with the kids and I don't care what I look like. I don't care what anyone says, I'm gonna cannonball with my great nephew even if the other adults say, "I'm not doing that." I don't care. He's four and if he wants Auntie Judy to do a cannonball and we'll have a contest and we'll do it.

It's fun because you only go around once. Why put up this front that I can only do this, I can only wear this, I can only say this, I can only walk this way? It's not really a way to live. That's my feeling anyways. I think it might be the direct result of what I went through because it makes you say, "Hmmmm."

When I was a young teenager, early 20s, I was smoking cigarettes and I was 21 and that's when I started running because I stopped smoking and I said, "Alright I need something else to fill my need." That's how I started running and I haven't stopped. I go two miles, three miles, whatever. Sometimes I run and I have to stop to walk because something hurts. I'm a little old, but I definitely feel better running, walking, skating—we just bought some kayaks so we go kayaking. Again, because you only go around once, I want to take full advantage of whatever's out there.

Samantha Vayo
Age 18
Interviewed on April 9, 2008 by Kimberly Powell of College of the Holy Cross; ASL Interpreters Rebekah Barton and Caitlin Scott of Northeastern University

I go to The Learning Center. It is a school for Deaf kids. My favorite class would have to be Math. I really love solving problems. My mom didn't find out I was deaf—I think I was around ten months old when my parents found out, so you know they don't know if I was born deaf or if [it was] right after I became really sick. I was born with CP [cerebral palsy], my parents told me I was born with CP and I went to the doctors and physical therapy and they told me that I would probably never walk. So, I proved them all wrong because I can walk, I like to play. I can do everything.

I've been involved in the Special Olympics since 1997, and I started competing in '98. I do gymnastics; I do soccer, bowling, baseball, and basketball. I have two favorites; the first is bowling and the second's gymnastics.

My mom first told me about it [modeling]. She asked me if I wanted to go and be in *Seventeen Magazine* and I was like "Of course I do!" So I filled out the application, I sent it in with my picture and they wrote me back, and they said, "Yes," they wanted me to go. They picked five girls out of 250 girls in the United States, but they only chose five girls. So of course I was so excited, I couldn't wait to go. So I went to New York and I was there for two days and it was so much fun! When I first got there they dyed my hair, I got to get all dressed up, they took before and after pictures, they took group photos, everything. Right now, I actually work in Boston as a model.

Anne Milkowski
Age 55
Interviewed on February 8, 2009 by Catherine Milkowski of Worcester State University

It was pretty ironic in the sense that just as I was finishing school and I thought I had climbed to the top of my mountain and got rid of the dark cloud over my head of this requirement that I couldn't keep my job until I finished school, I found a lump in my breast that seemed to have grown very quickly. But it had been a very stressful year the year before, with finishing up school and the incredible amount of paperwork involved. The year before when I had been to the doctor, I had joked about it being so easy to give myself breast exams because I had such small breasts. On my way out of the doctor's I was thinking if I ever had breast cancer it would certainly be ironic, because I had never really experienced having normal sized breasts and that would certainly be a very cruel twist of fate for me to get it. Well sure enough I got it, and I could always sort of tell going through the tests that—some of the tests would come out negative and I would have to go for one more, and it was so anchored that I knew in my heart it wasn't just a cyst. So I had to go for a mastectomy. And at first I thought, "Well, I can get through this if I don't have to go to chemo [chemotherapy] after." And then the first news was that I wouldn't have to do chemo, but I was very shortly told no, that wouldn't be the case, they had looked at the slide again and changed the diagnosis and I would have to have chemo. And again, juggling work and family and chemo was a trick too.

My daughter was] five years old, in kindergarten. So that was a difficult year anyway, because being a half-day program, as opposed to preschool being full day, for a working mom it's the most difficult year. I thought I had set up a babysitter here it would be okay, but she was not working out well for a variety of reasons, and then here I am with cancer and her quitting. Fortunately a better babysitter worked out, however I had to leave school and transport [her]. It worked out only on a fluke that I happened to have a planning period then, so it wasn't like…which I made up, it wasn't like they gave me time off to do this, but at least it got us through that year. When I was on the chemo, it was timed that I got sick on the weekends. I got treatment on a Thursday, have a half a day on Friday with some easier activity planned, and again because I lived so close to school

I could do it. If I had been driving an hour I probably couldn't have even done that. But however, it meant that I would be sick on the weekend and as chemo goes it gets worse as you go along. So the first couple weren't too bad and it got a little more difficult as it went along. But then by February it was done. Thought I was through, but in October I got the flu and on a checkup the doctor had discovered a lymph node had enlarged. For some reason she waited a whole month before biopsying it, but it did turn out to be cancerous and at that point they did some scans and I don't want to go into too many details on that because it ended up being a wash, but because of it being my second time, because of being young and healthy, having just finished PE [Physical Education] school, I did get referred to a program at Dana Farber [Cancer Institute] that was experimental.

It was quite daunting to look at how much was involved in the program because it was going to take nearly six months. Many steps, extremely aggressive. The point of the project was to find the maximum survivable dose of particular drugs, implies they are going to push the envelope pretty far. I had to sign—it was such an intense program I had to sign every page of the document of the proposal to make [sure that] I knew what I was getting into. They made it perfectly clear that they would take me down to have no immune system and that deciding to leave the program partway through would not be an option. It was very terrifying to think of who was going to take care of [my daughter]. That fell into place with [my husband] taking half sick time and landing a babysitter who had changed her college schedule just coincidentally before that happened, but I was back and forth. I didn't go in there for the full-time, I would go there for a few days and go home. It was preceded by so-called standard treatment at a local hospital, which was pretty difficult in and of itself. But it meant that I left school in February and didn't get out of the hospital until coincidentally the last day of school that year.

It was [difficult going back to work] because I was bald and I had to wear a wig and I hated my wig and it hurt. I am a very tactile defensive person so it's hard for me to ignore things and it felt like I had a rubber band on my head, and just a year, two years before that I had returned to work with severe shoulder pain and limited movement so it certainly made work difficult. For the first couple of years after the transplant I survived by not thinking about things, and my energy level was still not close to normal for a couple of years so it impacted a lot of things. My own bone marrow was not affected, so it was called an autologous transplant where they harvested the bone marrow, harvested stem cells prior to two rounds of extremely high dose chemo, so it wasn't really a transplant like getting somebody else's organ, but I am still considered a transplant survivor in that sense.

The first couple of years [of this experience of getting cancer], if I heard people talking about how much they are putting into retirement I—one time it made me cry at work while I was trying to do grades. I could hear these people and I just, I couldn't think that far ahead. I was just so jealous of them. It forced me to save heavily for my daughter's college because I wasn't sure if I'd be there to pay for it and I saved less for my own retirement because at that time I wasn't expected to have one. So it affected me that way. I think I was more—it was stronger at first, that I would hear people talking about silly things like a bad hair day, and if you've been bald you never have a bad hair day again. If you have hair, it's a pretty good day. A few times people made strange comments to me about, "Oh, well, you'd just be happy to be here," whereas they think they are entitled to some other level of activity and happiness, so that was always strange. For a few years you are very afraid to make plans for fear that the cancer is going to come back and it's going to be more heartbreaking because you can't live up to your plans. But as time went on, I started to look more towards the future, get less afraid of planning.

Pat Masiello
Age 73
Interviewed on February 24, 2011 by Charlene L. Martin

[My mother] was at the Senior Housing at Webster Square. Physically, she was pretty good. Mainly just dementia—she was a pretty darn healthy lady. The decision had to be made to take her with me or put her in a nursing home. She was in her late 70s or early 80s when I took her with me. And at that time it was more convenient seeing I was now separated from my husband and my sister had a family and my brother was out in Michigan. So it was much more convenient for me to have her with me than my sister or brother. She could get around well, she just—dementia had taken over so you forget when to eat, you forget if it's morning or night so I'd put her to bed and she'd be up 15 minutes later watching TV not realizing it's one or two o'clock in the morning.

But then fortunately I discovered that there was daycare and I was working full-time and I took her to daycare for several years and that worked out wonderfully at the Jewish Center on my way to work. [I'd] get her dressed and out of the house until the time came when she wouldn't get up for me. She just became very stubborn and decided what she didn't want to do. Well, then the siblings stepped in and they said it's too much for me to handle and maybe we should think about a nursing home. Well that took a while, but then it came to that eventually. She went to several.

I think she was 96 when she died and I think in the nursing home—maybe four or five years. She was a pretty healthy lady. She'd go through spills in the nursing home and come out of it fine. It was very difficult at times. And work—sometimes work is a salvation though because I don't think I would have wanted to stay home all day and deal with it. With Alzheimer's I think you have to start lying to them and not feel bad about it. And my sister had a lot of trouble with that. She battled trying to tell her and then two weeks later it doesn't work out. So you have to wind up fibbing. You're not hurting them and after a while you accept it too, but my sister, Polly, had a lot of trouble with that. I said, "Polly you're wasting your breath, you know. It's not going to happen." So she got the gist of it after a while and it is hard to fib to your parents, but it's for their benefit. It was very frustrating. Sometimes you want to pound the wall [laughs].

And during the middle of this, of course, was when my daughter [Donna] got sick. That was a shocker. She had two little kids. And she happened to call me one day and said, "I seem to be having some kind of hemorrhage here." Anyway, you go to your gynecologist and they tend to pooh-pooh, you know, our female problems—"Oh, just go home and we'll see how this goes." Well, it didn't go well. She was 34. Her children were six and nine, just six and nine.

They didn't seem to be too compassionate towards female problems at all. Just keep pooh-poohing, giving her a pill here, let's wait until next month, and on and on. And all the time this ends up being a serious problem. She had cervical cancer.

The rest of that year was spent between operations and thinking they're very successful and giving her a complete hysterectomy and you know, trying everything possible at that time. So it started in '94, April of '94. And through many operations, chemo, and radiation and all that, it just wasn't working. And at that time, I was taking the kids 'cause her husband has to work. So the two little ones were staying at my house—well they weren't that little. They were in school so I would take them to school on my way to work. They would sleep mostly at my house.

I tried to visit every single day, sometimes twice a day because after a while, after the operations and—she wound up being at a nursing home. And at that time nursing homes were just changing over to rehab [rehabilitation] and taking younger people. She went in around Thanksgiving and never came out. February—she died on February 2nd. That was '95.

I think I had my mother so long with me, you know, it was kind of a system I got into, a rhythm. With Donna, well this is very different. You do get—in looking back now I think I took it one day at a time because you had her children, work, and her. And then my mother, but with my mother I was in such a routine that—maybe she took a big backseat or maybe my sister helped me out somewhat. But Donna was my main concern and the children. So I think you kind of take one thing at a time.

So I think the hard times were in the nursing home, getting there before I go to work, getting there on my lunch hour, and getting there after work. There were a lot of visits. I mean you never know how much time you have.

Everybody handles it in their own way. And what I didn't realize until a few years ago is everybody is different. I didn't realize how it affected my son because you become very selfish. You think of yourself and the kids—the little kids. You don't think of anybody else really. I mean, her husband certainly must have had a different feeling, my son, my daughter-in-law, and an ex-daughter-in-law—I never realized how she felt.

Yet the father kind of swept them away very quickly. They disappeared from my house. He needed them. And he said that, "I need them." Again he didn't give thought to me like I didn't give thought to him, but I'd had them, you know. Well at least six months they slept at my house. Getting them dressed for school, taking them to school, pick them up after school. It was like having two kids taken away from you. It was really a hole that was left after he grabbed them. Naturally there was a lot of times I had to do things for them. They still need you. They need somebody. It's been a good experience. Naturally it's not one we would choose, but I'm glad that I've been in the same state and available to them. Not sure how they feel about it. [Laughs]

All of a sudden, after [my sister, Polly's] retirement from Mass Academy [Massachusetts Academy for Math and Science], she found out she had liver cancer. And again, like Donna's, nine months later she was gone from us. [Polly and I] were very close. As youngsters, as I said, she was my pain in the neck as younger sisters are. Once you've grown up and have families and children we were very close. There's nothing like a sister. Brothers are okay, but it's just not the same. [Laughs] She was 63, 63.

It was just—it's hard to lose—it's hard to reminisce with anybody else about your childhood once you lose a sibling. Your parents are gone. I did have my brother, Ed. He's in Michigan and Arizona. But there are things you have no one else to talk to about once your siblings are gone. And then best friends also. I've lost a couple of best friends. So it's hard even if you make new friends, there's no history there. You lose a lot of your history when you lose your family members. "Do you remember Dad doing that? Do you remember Mom doing that?" There is no one to ask that anymore.

And my two best girlfriends that I grew up with—especially Mary Lou—I lost her and we were friends at Dix Street from the time we were ten years old. So we had a lot to reminisce about. A lot. And so when you lose your very best friend of which few of us have more than one or two of those, it—the realization that life is getting shorter. [Laughs] So write your memories down. [Laughs]

I think that our paths are cut somewhere. You know everyone says, "Is there a reason that this happened?" And I never really asked that reason. I do believe there was a reason that Donna died and that I had my mother living with me. I'm still working on my sister [laughs]. But I think as you get older you can almost see that somebody had a journey for you and this is it. I think that's why you have to live in the day. Because there was always a new day. You go to bed thinking, "Oh God, I can't go through this again." And then a day or two later—maybe it's not always the next day—but you're given a different day. If you've got patience and you can wait, you are given a new day.

Lori Connolly
Age 33
Interviewed on February 28, 2009 by Stephanie Dudek of Worcester State University

When you are an occupational therapist, you can work with kids, you can work with adults, you can work outpatient, you can do geriatrics. At that time, there were usually more jobs with geriatrics and I ended up working in a nursing home, sub-acute. Meaning patients don't stay there forever. They go, they get better, and they go home. It was good, but you know, I was there for six months and I got a pay cut. After already being there for six months because of all the changes that [were] happening because of Medicare, but a lot of that has been changed. Most of those regulations don't exist and OT is flourishing again and now they don't have enough of occupational therapists.

I have a lot of responsibilities. My daughter, one of my daughters has cerebral palsy. And, so, she requires a lot of attention and time because she can't do things herself, that at four and a half, almost five years old, [she] should be able to do. She's come a long way from where she was, but she still needs help most of the time. She can get herself dressed but she still needs help sometimes, not so much with feeding but getting on the toilet, getting off the toilet, brushing her teeth, putting on her shoes, putting on her socks, and walking. Which is a huge thing, plus not only that, being an occupational therapist, there is a ton more pressure on me to—I know, I'm almost too much. So, I know that if she's going to walk, then this is the time to do it. I may come home [from work] and work with her for a couple hours, spend a little time with her sister. Or have [her sister] do the exercises with us. Most of my time is either working, doing [my daughter's] therapy, taking care of the kids, cleaning the house—which is low on the priority list, to be honest with you—and researching online, all the time, to see what's out there. You know, like going into a chat room. I belong to a chat room for people who have CP (cerebral palsy). Could be adults, kids, parents. I spend a lot of time on there just kind of figuring out what is out there for people. I should probably mention my husband in there. I spend a little time with him. [Laughter] I do spend some time with him as well. But you know I don't really go out; I don't have time for leisure. I do go to the gym in the morning, so I do balance that. I do belong to the Leicester Parent Advisory Council. Which is a special education advisory council for the special education department of Leicester and I'm the vice chair.

I feel that I work really hard for the money I have and I feel that any extra money that I have, goes directly to my daughter. I don't get any help, I don't get any money from the Department of Mental Retardation; I don't get any money from the Department of Public Health. I don't get any of that money that a lot of other families get due to income. I'm not complaining. It's just that I'm just very lucky I have the job that I do and I can pick up extra hours to make the money that I feel that my daughter deserves and the opportunities that she deserves in order to be able to independently walk, but I am little nervous that my taxes may change or my benefits may change what I have.

Ann Klump
Age 65
Interviewed on October 12, 2006 by Sarah Ciras of Worcester State University

Three-quarters of my ancestors came over in 1635, probably mostly from England. And then my maternal grandmother came over and—when she was nine—and she's of Latvian descent. My mother was born and brought up in Worcester, lived here all her life. Her father grew up very poor in western Massachusetts, Ludlow, near Springfield. My mother was the only one that went to a private school – she went to Mount Holyoke. She tried teaching and hated it. My mother stayed home [after marriage] and took care of us. She did go back to work when I was in high school, and she worked as a social worker [for the] Worcester City Missionary Society. At that time, the social workers working for the state were really— their hands were tied on what they could say. So, my mother had more flexibility on what she could talk about, like birth control. She would work with large families and thought they were struggling.

There was the polio epidemics. That I remember 'cause I got non-paralytic polio so I was in the hospital with some of the children who were in iron lungs. It didn't affect me as much as other people.

My husband's health issues have impacted me a lot. My husband has epilepsy. He's had it since birth. He didn't have seizures for a while, he had very small ones, but that has kept him from driving. I've had to drive him places. More recently, he's had some issues with manic depression, which has some medication that cause more issues than the disease. Every time they try to take away some of the medications he ends up with a battery of five seizures, has to go into the hospital for the day, and then for rehab [rehabilitation]. And we get this whole thing where his balance is off, can't walk as well, using a walker, he has to have help with the shower. That's had an impact, a big impact. My issues have been temporary. I had a broken leg the weekend before I was starting my new job with the dentist. Because he was a skier, he just let me come to work in a cast for eight months. I think my own health issues haven't really affected me as much—they're minor.

Patricia Donovan
Age 58
Interviewed on April 4, 2006 by Melissa Whiting of Worcester State University

[My daughter] was talking a blue streak when she was 12 months old, always questioning things, she was singing and dancing and acting when she was six. She was really an amazing woman who really had one of those personalities that was mentally ill. So, she fell apart. She had bipolar illness when she was 19.

Well, my daughter has a mental illness, that has been a huge factor. That has really driven a lot of what I do—taking care of her, supporting her so that she could be a mother, and functioning independently. I had to be very available for my granddaughter because my daughter has a major mental illness. So, I helped raise [her]. I've always had her one night a week overnight. It gives her mother a break.

My own illness is starting to creep up with my leg problems. I really hate it. I don't like being slowed down. It's made me gain weight...I've got this pain in my leg for two and a half years ago this month—in my knee. I didn't know what it was. Jack told me to go have it looked at and they did an x-ray or an MRI [Magnetic Resonance Imaging] or whatever and they said, "Oh, you have a torn meniscus. You need arthroscopic surgery." I went and had that done and ever since then, I've had more horrible problems than I did before. Horrible. The physical therapy caused a problem in my walking which is, just now, this week, they've discovered how to treat it. In the meantime, I had a second surgery. They found I had arthritis in my knees so they started to do that. It's really slowed me down. I really hate that I can't walk—I always was a walker. I would walk probably two to three miles a day. It really changes—this issue, the pain in my knee—has changed my day-to-day routine a lot.

When I was 13, I lost my best friend .... She had strep throat. It spread through her body and it was untreated. Nowadays when someone gets a sore throat, you say go to the doctors to get a culture—they didn't do that then. They had just started to do that. She died. I never really got over that. And then in two years, [my friend] Susan died who had a heart problem and she had heart surgery and she died on the table. Never would've happened today. This was 1958 or something.

I think the most grief that I've experienced was when I realized how sick my daughter was. She wasn't going to graduate from Rutgers, she wasn't going to have a normal—I realized in high school there was something really wrong. As years have gone on, I've had to constantly realize and feel grief. When your kid doesn't grow up to do all of the things that you expect, there's a constant sense of loss. The loss of my family when I got divorced, that was huge. Then the next sense of loss—this is interesting—

menopause. I went into menopause very early. I thought, "Well, it isn't time yet. What's happening here?" That was very difficult. That took a couple of years and therapy. My body changed a lot. I was about 42. I had a climbing accident ... and when I was recovering, I was realizing that there was hormonal changes going on and all that kind of stuff. Your fluids change. I lost my tears. I had dry eye so I couldn't wear contacts so I had to wear glasses. Then I gained a lot of weight, I quit smoking. When I quit smoking and went into menopause I gained a lot of weight. A lot. I look in the mirror and I still don't know who I am. You have a different sense of yourself as a sexual being and start to be not—sort of anonymous with men. They just look through you. I definitely sense that....It's a very strange experience. It's definitely a transition—there's definitely grief involved and loss.

Alexandria Phillips
Age 22
Interviewed on April 19, 2006 by Briana Roy of Worcester State University

     I'm part Irish. I have a very strong Irish history and culture instilled in me through my mother. I believe in a lot of Irish folklore and Irish beliefs and I really feel that is something that has been instilled in me. It is something that I want to instill further in my life with my children and throughout my life. I also have some Native American in me.
     Illness has played an extreme role in my life. Physical illness, mental illness—not only in my own life, but in my nuclear family. As far as I'm concerned, my mother's side of the family has extreme chemical imbalances. I, from a very early age, the age of four, started showing signs of extreme, extreme anxiety attacks. By the age of six, I was

having about 30-35 anxiety attacks a day. And when my mother sought help from physicians, it was claimed that I was a quote unquote anxious child with separation issues from my parents. No one realized in the '80s that there were medicines that could help severe chemically induced anxiety. It was nothing of my doing, nothing that I could control or that my parents could control. To this day, my anxiety is a lot better.

I never received any treatment as a child for my anxiety. I couldn't keep my food down due to my high anxiety levels. At the age of about 13, my mother really being the only person who could relate to my anxiety issues due to her own anxiety issues, basically told me that I either needed to get better on my own or I would die due to the fact that I couldn't eat. Being at the age of 13, it really wasn't within my power to go out and seek my own help. I was kind of in a powerless situation, so I kind of took the mind over matter thing, and force fed myself and started to build some weight. The anxiety didn't go away, but presently the anxiety plays a lower role in my life and I do have better control over it. It's not induced, it's not social anxiety, it's all chemical based. It happens at very random times for no reason whatsoever.

Body image for me personally has never been an issue. Growing up I've always been extremely tall, I'm currently six feet tall. So, being thin and being tall is very recognizable. I was judged by many, many outside sources—adults, students, peers—[to be] anorexic and that wasn't the case at all. As I got older and started gaining weight I never had a problem with body image. I was happy and content with finally being able to eat and in that sense being able to live a normal life with food. When I went to college—the freshman 15, I gained a substantial amount of weight when I went to Framingham State College. You're not eating healthy and you're not eating the way you should and that was an issue for my mother. She would tell me that

I needed to lose weight and that I was getting chunky and my appearance has always been very important to my mother, for herself, for me, and for her husband, my father, as well. When we go out, we have to look like the perfect family, and we have to—if I wasn't wearing clothes that weren't exactly flattering to my figure when I was going through my heavier period, she'd definitely point it out.

Other health issues I've had—I've suffered from extreme depression, also chemically induced. So I've fought a lot of illness mentally throughout my life and being sick mentally also causes you to be sick physically, be weak, physically weak, just not up for the challenges of every day. So, yes, mental and physical illness have played a large role in my life thus far.

Suzanne Lewandowski
Age 55
Interviewed on November 10, 2009 by Erin Muschette and Eily Finn of Assumption College

My only challenges were related to the eating disorder. When you develop an eating disorder it takes over your life, it interferes with your emotional health, physical health, psychological health, your ability to concentrate on a job or your studies and …it's very difficult to recover from. I suffered from bulimia for 25 years. I developed it at 19, within a few weeks after the death of my father, and I have only been recovered since 1999…so I wasted about 25 years of my life. For all practical purposes there were several times I should have died. I have survived and I have a voice that can help.

I hid it very well for the first, well the first ten years I had it. The word bulimia hadn't even, well I'm sure it existed, but it had never been in the public eye. My eating disorder started in January of 1974, at least the bulimia did. It was in the '80s when I first heard the word—when I realized that I was not the only one in the world that had this horrible problem. But by then it was so enmeshed in my everyday living that I couldn't stop and I stopped trying to stop.

An eating disorder doesn't just happen on a diet, it is a, it's like a puzzle, the pieces here and there come together and you start poking in a certain direction and the pieces fill in maladaptive behaviors. In my case, my mother had cancer when I was growing up. She had depression because of it, which turned into mental illness. So, my mother's relationship and mine is very difficult and then when my ex-husband came into the picture I was torn and torn in two again. So, when you are already down that path, you already have problems with relationships and when every minute is spent thinking about food, or eating, or finding the bathroom to throw it up, it gets really difficult to maintain relationships especially when you don't want anybody to know.

I look at things as a jigsaw puzzle and I have a lot of pieces—well in my own recovery during the process of that 25 years I developed alcoholism. I was a pretty hard alcoholic for about five years, and I've been sober now for 16 and a half years, and in sobriety I've learned how to cope with life on life's terms and gradually rebuild the puzzle of my life.

Back in 2003, I was asked to be PTA [Parent Teacher Association] President of a [school] in North Brookfield. I had never been a leader in anything in my life, and it was a very terrifying year. It was the best year and the worst year of my life. I learned how to face anxiety, to follow through, and to make a difference.

There are no facilities in the Worcester County that treat eating disorders. There are maybe four or five nutritionists, maybe five or six therapists. I have yet to find a primary care physician that specializes in eating disorders. And so, my goal is to bring services to Worcester County to treat people with eating disorders because they are most successfully treated with early diagnosis. When college students leave, they will not get well unless they get help.

I have people calling me all the time looking for services and when you have an eating disorder you're in a cocoon that you can't get out of, you just...your life is horrible, it's—it's just the quality of life is devastating emotionally and psychologically and physically and...I think I have to help, I have no choice. You know there's—there's just no question about it. I have a voice now and I'm not going to let these young kids spend 25 years doing what I did.

Wilma Sanchez
Age 47
Interviewed on March 24, 2011 by Maureen Ryan Doyle and Charlene L. Martin

I was born in Puerto Rico. I was born in Hato Rey and then I was raised in Caimito. And the reason for that was because when I was born, my mother wouldn't take me. So my grandparents, my father, and my aunt were the ones who raised me until I was six years old. When I was six, my mother came. And I don't know, she made an arrangement with my father. My father refused to give her any money unless she would raise me. So at the age of six I went to live with my mother and my father also.

When I went to live with her, she used to work in a bar in Puerto Rico. My mother was more like, gee I don't think she had a clue what it was like to be a mother, you know, now that I think about it today. She was more...she was very flirtatious. She was always flirting with someone. I want to say that I was almost seven, she used to.... my father got her a house and he would go to work, and in the mornings this man that lived up the hill from behind the house used to come down the hill and would talk to my mother. And he would give my mother something. You know, today I strongly believe it was money. And then she would call me outside and tell me to go with the man. And I would go up the hill with the man up to his house and he would put a plate of Oreo cookies, a little small plate, and then he would put milk. And then he would pick me up and put me on top of the counter. He would tell me to have some and then he would grab the plate and the milk and walk me to a little shed behind the house. And he used to molest me when I was a kid. And to this day I hate Oreo cookies. I'm not having Oreo cookies because of that. And that used to happen, I don't know, numerous times during the week. And I never told my father. I never told anybody, any adult, anyone older.

The first state that I came to in the United States was Manchester, New Hampshire....that's where I learned how to speak English. I graduated sixth grade and my mother left my father for another man. We ended up moving to Manhattan. I was 12 and a half, almost 13. And I was...at that age I was already built. You know, I had a body. And these men used to touch me and I would tell them no. They used to tell me, "Don't tell your mother because she is not going to believe you. And if you tell, I'm going to tell you're lying." My mother was real sneaky. And she was making an arrangement with the man from the store because the man wanted to send for his brother from Santo Domingo. He needed to marry his brother with a citizen in order for him to get his green papers. And I don't know how this came out, but my mother said that he could marry me. And the deal was, the man was going to give her $5,000, half of that when we would get married, the other half when he would get his papers. I ended up running away and calling my sister in Lowell, Mass. I ended up going over to my ex-brother-in-law who lived in Lynn, Mass. I stayed there with his family and his sister. He was like a brother to me. He took care of me. Nobody knew where I was.

So I ended up being with [a] man—we grew up together when we were kids. Being with this man was one of the biggest mistakes because I found out that he was an alcoholic. So here I am a teenager, a kid, I was smoking weed, I was doing mescaline, I was drinking alcohol, and we were partying every weekend. I was 13, 14. I ended up getting pregnant from him. I ended up getting pregnant at the age of 15. But every weekend, no lie, every weekend I had a black eye. Because I was a kid and he wanted me to cook. And I didn't know how to cook. My mother never taught me how to cook; she only wanted me to clean. So, he would come home and if the rice wasn't done right or if the potatoes weren't cooked right, he threw them against the living room wall. And I would get beat up. He would go every weekend to the bar and because of his mouth, he would always get beat up by men at the bar. And he would come home and say it was my fault.

But it was that vicious cycle. I was constantly trying to numb my feelings. I was always drinking or smoking or taking mescaline. It was always something. I started working at this factory. And I used to work the graveyard shift, the third shift. And I met a Colombian guy there and he used to sell cocaine. I tried it, so every night he would bring me cocaine and I would sniff it. Then [pause] I ended up getting in a relationship with my brother's best friend, who happens to be my son's father today. Well, anyways that didn't last too long because he was a drug dealer and he was having sex with a bunch of other women. He was paying them with drugs. So he had…while I got pregnant, he had another woman pregnant at the same time. So it just seemed like my whole life was always getting hurt. And I ended up in this relationship with my best friend, who was a female. Let me tell you something, there's no difference, man woman, there's no difference. It was a vicious cycle.

Then her parents came and got me and took me to Connecticut ... so that I would get better when they found out what I was doing because they loved my kids. And that was the worst thing that could have happened because down there I met people I should have never met. I met this woman ... and she taught me the ropes, she taught me how to work the streets. My disease of addiction had progressed from one day to another. The minute I shot up that cocaine I fell in love with it. So in order to calm down from the cocaine, I met this guy who told me to do heroin, you know, it'll bring you down. So then I started doing the heroin.

I injected somebody's blood in my body who is HIV [Human Immunodeficiency Virus] positive. I knew, but I didn't want to know. And I ended up getting really sick. I ended up with Hepatitis B. They did an AID's [Acquired Immune Deficiency Syndrome] test. They gave me a number and I threw it away. I didn't want to know. I was so desperate that I wanted to die after being raped so many times, being sexually abused so many times. I begged God to please help me.

I ended up in [Massachusetts Correctional Institution] Framingham. I was in jail for prostitution. I was desperate, so I started calling places. I got clean; I went to Spectrum [Health Systems]. And I remember going to DSS [Department of Social Services], fighting for my kids and this man who worked at DSS, right in downtown, said to me, "Why do you want your son if you're going to die? You've got HIV." This is one of the reasons I came to work in the field of Human Service, 'cause I couldn't understand how somebody could be so cold. Anyways, I worked at Spectrum after two and a half years of getting clean. I ended up going to Springfield College. I went there for a Bachelor's

[Degree]. And I just couldn't stop there. I kept going. Unfortunately everything I do, I do to the extreme. [Laughter] I kept going and I got my Master's [Degree] ... I finished in 2009 and graduated in May, 2010. I did the program at Westfield State College to become a certified counselor, the C.A.C. program. I got my LADC I, licensed addiction drug counselor.

I educated my kids and I'm HIV, and I've been living with HIV for 25 years ... and if I don't tell you, you'll never know. I'm healthy to this day, thank God. And I'm going on 15 years, June 30, clean. I am a clinician, a substance abuse counselor at Habit OPCO. I love what I do. I just have a passion. I don't know, I guess God knew what He was doing.

Ann McCarron
Age 45
Interviewed on April 18, 2008 by Katherine DeMarco and Meredith Morris of Assumption College

I would love to tell you my story—it's a story that began when I was seven years old. I had a disease called rheumatic fever and Saint Vitus Dance. And I was a little girl down the Cape [Cod] with my grandmother and I kept falling and this is what they ended up finding. I had this disease and it affects your nervous system. So then my Grandmother took me to my parents and they rushed me into a hospital in Boston, and they entrusted this person to take care of me and make me healthy. What they didn't know was that this pediatrician was a person that was going to sexually abuse me for the next five years. From there I ended up developing migraine headaches and I was hospitalized in private rooms and that's when I was sexually abused by this pediatrician.

Back then my parents would put the doctor on a pedestal and because he helped me, but they didn't know that and I was confused. I never said anything. I was numb and I was told by him that I would go to jail if I ever said anything and I never did until 25 years later. I went through years of therapy and figured out who I was and how I survived as a little girl. And I had a Dad and a Mom that were over protective and would have done anything to protect me but they didn't know. I also had my Dad, you know, at night when I would go to bed [he] would say, "Goodnight princess, sweet dreams." I had loving parents and three brothers. I couldn't walk down the street without them watching me and knowing where I was all the time.

And then from there, after going through years of therapy and figuring out how the child sexual abuse affected me, I ended up realizing that it did affect me ... and how I survived. I talk about the basketball coach—he was this basketball coach I had in junior high school—he looked at me and said, "McCarron, you could be the best basketball player you want to be." And I took that and that's when [I] ran [with it] and I had the desire. Looking back those are the things, the tools I needed to survive and it gave me my self-esteem, you know, that I was successful at something. This abuse wasn't putting me down. From there I started working recreation and that's probably why I love sports.

I did do some research after therapy to find out [who] this pediatrician was and all I remember that when I was growing up that he was caught, and I thought he went to jail. So I did want to make him accountable and I hired a private investigator in New Hampshire. And I discovered he has fled the country and he was no longer practicing medicine. So that was good. And so I went to see some lawyers and that my case came to an end with the statute of limitations, but I still felt the effects of child abuse. So what I ended up doing was putting together a project ten years ago called *Bike Across America—Voices for Children.*

I went to Assumption College [employer], to our administrators, and I asked them to support me for this cause. And I wanted to cycle across the country to break the silence of child sexual abuse. They said, "You can have 50 days off, you can do this," and that changed my life. And I didn't own a bike before I did this so. [Laughs] I got everything donated. I asked for support—Coca-Cola gave me a van in San Diego to help me move my gear and I had the [Assumption College] Reach Out Center students help me during the journey, my Mom and Dad came with me and helped different times. People would fly in and out and help me ride, support me, and get the TV interviews and newspapers because what we wanted to do—ten years ago it wasn't on the front page of the paper. People had a hard time listening to the stories or they didn't believe them. So a lot has happened since ten years ago. And when I got back, when I finished here at Assumption College, [that] was one of the most memorable days of my life.

I realized it wasn't a one-time event, that the journey continues. And we have an annual bike ride except I'm not going across the country again. [Laughs] And I ask other people to join in and as a community [for] all of us to reach out, but more importantly, I think my story changed and we know about it and now [that] we know about it, what are we doing about it? And the difference is we can empower our children to speak up.

I guess when I look back now, is that we all have different roles in our lives. What I mean by that is, I'm a recreation director, I have a son. I'm a mom. I have friends, but the most important role is my role as a mom. And it's one of the most challenging roles of raising a child, and I look at him and I think about you know how is he going to be safe when I drop him off, when I bring him to baseball, who's his coach, who's he working with, where, when he goes to camp? Even when I tuck him into bed at night, you wonder and you hope he's going to be safe. And now I think when I grew up we could play out in the streets but the difference now is we have parents that are out there. There are "helicopter moms," they call them, you know, and everyone is trying to protect their kids. Like my parents did that, but with child sexual abuse, it's usually someone you know and trust. It's usually someone you know and trust.

It's very powerful how they manipulate, how they are, but the difference is what I can do with Quinn. And when I look at him now, I flash back and I remember myself as—Quinn is almost going to be seven now—I look back at him and I flash back and I think about how when I was a little girl. The difference is I'm teaching him to speak up for himself. Not to be afraid to tell me something that is confusing or secret and to be able to say, "No," because it is on the front page. I think that's a good thing now, we need to get the message out there that kids need because we're not going to be with them 24/7.

So I mean that's kind of where I've grown and learned and developed who I was and how it affected me. And also, other victims have come up to me for the first time and told me their story. People have called me and told me about, you know, "My grandfather just passed away and I've had this secret. And now I can finally say something." And I encourage victims to go from being a victim to a victor in life. And I hope to empower other women and children and parents to not be afraid to speak out about child sexual abuse.

And I hope I can encourage other victims to make the choices and continue to work, but you need to ask for that support and help. I do go out and speak about it. And I don't consider myself an expert, but I also consider myself a person somebody can put a face to a victim. As that little girl, you can hear it in my voice, and it doesn't take a lot for me to get that emotion back.

I also think of my parents, I never want anyone to go through what my parents have gone through ever since I told them about the abuse. Because they would have done anything to protect me, but they didn't know.

CHAPTER FIVE

POLITICS/COMMUNITY INVOLVEMENT

"But to those who believe in having a government-to those who believe that no government can be formed without the consent of the governed-to them I would appeal, and of them do I demand some good reason why one half of the citizens of this Republic have no voice in the laws which govern them."

From Elizabeth Cady Stanton, Seneca Falls, NY, October 20, 1850—Read in the morning session on October 24, 1850, in Worcester, MA

The political status of women in the United States at the time of the First National Woman's Rights Convention was a highly debated topic. Dissatisfaction with the limited opportunities for work and inability to vote, stirred the consciousness of many. However, there were also those who did not want to extend the vote to women. Some were concerned that it would mean the end of the family structure and men would lose control of their wives. Some thought that women simply were not capable of understanding the complexities of issues upon which they would be asked to cast a ballot. Some even feared that suffrage for women would be an affront to God Himself.

The political battle for women's suffrage was waged for many years. The accounts of the strength and determination of those early suffragists are well documented. They include Elizabeth Cady Stanton's statement, "All men and women are created equal," in her *Declaration of Rights and Sentiments*; Lucy Stone clearly elucidating, "I must speak for the women," in a speech in 1847; and Sojourner Truth, a former slave, who delivered her famous *Ain't I A Woman* speech at a women's rights convention in Ohio in 1851. In the speech she listed all the things that she could do equal to or better than a man.

During the 19th century many women became involved in reform movements aimed at the abolition of slavery and the banning of alcohol. In the hearts and minds of several early suffragists, there existed great similarities between the plights of slaves and those of wives. Neither group had a voice or power over their own lives. Some women were supporters of the temperance movement because they saw a link between alcohol-consuming husbands and the poverty to which many of their families were subjected.

Winning the vote did not come easily, but there were victories to be celebrated in the midst of the struggle. In 1869 the Territory of Wyoming passed the first women's suffrage law, and in 1870 women began to serve on juries there. In 1893 Colorado became the first state to adopt an amendment granting women the right to vote. Finally, on August 26, 1920, the 19th amendment to the U.S. Constitution was passed, granting women throughout the United States the right to vote. In 1922 women voted in their first federal election.

With suffrage now a guaranteed right, opportunities for women broadened and so did women's goals and aspirations. In 1916 Jeanette Rankin of Montana became the first woman elected to the U.S. House of Representatives. In 1968, Shirley Chisholm of New York was the first African-American woman elected to the U.S. House. Hattie Caraway of Arkansas was appointed in 1932 to the U.S. Senate and then elected in 1933. From 1949 until 1973 Margaret Chase Smith served the state of Maine as U.S. Senator. Frances Perkins was the first female Cabinet member. She served as Secretary of Labor under President Franklin D. Roosevelt.

The presidential election of 1980 marked the first time that women voters outnumbered men. While progress in the political arena has been substantial, it is important to note that the number of women holding public office in this country is still far less than the number of men who serve in this capacity. In this chapter you will encounter three women who have achieved great success in politics: a current State Senator, a former State Representative, and the first female mayor of the city of Worcester. While some women pursue careers in politics, others choose to become politically active by means of their volunteer efforts within their community. Several of their stories are presented here as well. We trust that you will find their commitment to serve to be inspiring, uplifting, and of great merit. As Senator Olympia Snowe of Maine stated so eloquently, "From the classroom to the workroom, the legislative changes pushed by women will touch the lives of most every woman and her family through expanded medical research on women's health, better protection against domestic violence, and improved social opportunities."

Massachusetts State Senator
Harriette Chandler
Age 73
Interviewed on August 10, 2010
by Maureen Ryan Doyle and
Charlene L. Martin

This was a very late career goal. I started as a teacher when that was one of the few jobs I could have gotten when I graduated from college. I went on to get a Master's Degree from Clark [Clark University] and they allowed me to go on for a Doctorate, a Ph.D. in International Relations and Government.

I taught at Clark, WPI [Worcester Polytechnic Institute], and Tufts [Tufts University]. I took a job as Executive Director of the National Women's Committees at Brandeis [University]. Then I decided I wanted my MBA [Master's Degree in Business Administration]. So, I've had a variety of jobs. That is not typical for someone my age. We never expected to work full-time—careers were not really expected.

My mother became quite ill and I quit my job to care for her. So I started reading the Worcester papers every day. There was great concern in 1990 about the fact that the schools were so bad that realtors were having trouble selling homes. I thought that maybe I could be of some help, so I decided to run for School Committee. The rest is history, as they say.

I served one and a half terms on the School Committee. I later served three terms in the House [State House of Representatives]. And then I ran for the Senate. It was a brutal race. It proved to me you could do anything you really want to do, if you work hard enough.

I served five terms in the Senate. I was the first woman to run from Worcester and win a Senate seat. I'm running now for my sixth term.

I've loved every moment of it. I love helping people. What better way of helping people than changing some of the laws under which they live. I have been very interested in senior citizens because the face of poverty for seniors is women. They live longer. We just passed a bill that will encourage people to buy long-term care insurance, particularly women, so they're not going to outlive their money.

Women are very hesitant to run for office. They start thinking about how much money they have to raise, they start wondering if they have enough of a base, they ask themselves if they have the right set of talents. Do they have the right degrees? We as women think we can solve everything by going to school and getting another degree. The truth of the matter is men don't think this way at all. They graduate from college, and if they want to run, they run. But women don't think that way. It's all got to be more carefully planned out. About a quarter of the Legislature are women and that is the same percentage we've had for the entire 16 years I've been there.

There are some bills that you deal with and you really agonize over them. And there are others where you know that you did the right thing. My rule of thumb, in bills involving conscience, I have to feel I can get up in the morning, look myself in the mirror and say, "This is the reason I voted the way I did and I'm comfortable with that." If I can't say that, I can't vote that way. And there are always bills like that.

Sara Robertson, First Female Mayor of Worcester, MA
Age 72
Interviewed on October 4, 2006 by Melanie Demarais and Linda Rosenlund

The first time I saw Worcester was from the window of a train. I had left California to go to Boston University graduate school. I looked around, all this smoke coming out of stacks, houses on top of houses, I had never seen anything like that before. It just to me was the worst environment I had ever seen. I found out I was very wrong. You can't judge a book by its cover.

The reason I got my arm twisted to run for City Council was the civic center. Our strategic location was so fabulous, seventh largest density population within a 50-mile radius of any city in the U.S. You can't beat that for a civic center. That is why ours has been so much more successful.

I had jobs with the Dukakis [Governor Michael Dukakis] administration, Assistant Secretary of Commerce and Central Massachusetts Regional Developer for Affordable Housing Initiative. The first thing I did when I arrived in Worcester was join the LWV [League of Women Voters]. I had joined in California, but I was having babies, so I was not a very active member. I found out how to join here and at the first meeting I walked into a room full of Sara Robertsons…."Boing! This is for me."

So I started some initiatives with the LWV, women to be observers at City Council meetings. I often was one of those observers. I loved that government was that close. I could sit down and watch it here. It was like the popularity of reality TV, watching the dynamics of reality. They are not playing games, they are really trying to survive.

I had been President of LWV and I went to City Council, so people were aware of me. Helen Bowditch and Christine Plumley said that they thought I would be a good person to run for school committee. You know, EGO ran...on the other hand, I've got a two year-old and a five and six year-old. I'm saying, "Hey wait a minute, what does it entail?"

Even though I had studied government and taught government, I had never been active in a campaign. Well once I got into it, I realized people were saying, "Sara who?" I had zero name recognition. I figured out that the only way I could get over this "Sara who" business was looking at precinct maps, looking at the voting list, and look at the neighborhoods and figure out where didn't know who I was. And go door to door. And that is what I did. Every two years I did that. I enjoyed it. Underneath the veneer is an encyclopedia salesperson. I like to go door to door and see what's going to appear. It was a challenge, entertaining, frustrating, and onerous. But I loved it.

Why did I decide to run? My kids were about to start Lee Street School, an old rundown brick building with a teeny playground. I was very concerned about the lack of libraries and the lack of extracurricular activities. I thought I could get on the School Committee and I could change it all around. And I quickly found out differently.

Did I make a difference? I followed my mentor Helen in being a consensus builder. The School Committee meetings used to be in City Hall back then. I thought we should get them out to the community. With a lot of prodding and pushing, one meeting a month would be at a school. We got tremendous support for that. Parents would come because it was right in their neighborhood. We were bringing government to the people.

When I was nine months pregnant, President of LWV, we ran a voter services drive. At that time the only place to register to vote was City Hall. I got the League behind me and the City Council behind me. Bob O'Keefe, City Clerk, was diametrically opposed to it. "If people can't bother to come to City Hall to register, they shouldn't vote," he said. The first night we went to Green Island and we had a big van with tables and chairs. The City Clerk said, "I won't do it. I thought I'd be in an office." This neighborhood center didn't have an office. I called [City Councilor] Joe Tinsley and he came to the neighborhood center and said, "Bob, we voted to allow this to happen, come on." Bob said, "No, I'm not going to do it." I got on the phone with Msgr. Harrington and I said, "Monsignor., we are having a problem down here at Green Island." We had a good bond, and I am not even a Catholic. He came down and said, "Bob O'Keefe, I think you want to go down there and register the people." And that is how it happened.

Yes, I did make a difference. And then we did this all over the city. It was great. I accomplished something that no one thought was possible of accomplishing.

Mary Jane McKenna
Age 67
Interviewed on November 13, 2006 by Andrew Whitmore and Mark Thomas of Assumption College

My sister was a nurse, so I decided I was going to be a nurse. And I went through all the tests, and I was accepted at a local hospital. I was supposed to go in August. In July I got the rules, regulations, and uniforms. And I said, "I don't want to be a nurse, I don't want to be a nurse." And I ended up going to Salter Secretarial School in Worcester. I graduated at the top of my class, and I took the first job I was offered.

I worked for two men in the insurance business. They influenced me as much as anybody. They were wonderful and they taught me a philosophy that I held for the rest of my life. "You do everything a little bit better, a little bit nicer than the next guy, and you will succeed."

I got married, stopped working, and had three children. I eventually went back to work for the town of Holden. I got a call one day from the Planning Board in Holden. They needed a part-time secretary. From there I worked for six or eight different boards in the town. I found out that I enjoyed town politics and I met a lot of wonderful people. And then I decided I knew as much as anybody. So I ran for the Board of Selectmen, and I was elected. I was the first woman.

I did that for six years. And then I got a call from our State Representative, Jim Harrington. He said that he was going to be resigning his seat and he decided that I was the one to succeed him. So I said, "What have I got to lose?" I was a Republican and I ran. I had a Democrat and an Independent that I ran against, and I clobbered them.

It was a wonderful district and I served in the Legislature for five full terms, and never had any opposition after that. I was elected for a sixth term, and one of my friends in the Legislature had just been elected to Congress. I was on his transition team and we were trying to find a District Director because he was having three offices in his congressional district. One day he walked up to me in the chamber and he said, "I've found my District Director, you." I said, "Why not?" So, I resigned my seat and I ran his offices from 1993 until 1995. And it was a good experience learning federal government.

When I was in the Legislature, the Republicans were the extreme minority. [Governor] Mike Dukakis was a very nice guy and he was planning to run for President, and he spent the state almost into bankruptcy because this was his way of building up constituencies. And Bill Weld came in and he did a phenomenal job. He was the best governor I've ever known. He put the state back in order.

Governor Bill Weld appointed me to the Massachusetts Office of Travel and Tourism as their Executive Director. And I served there for seven years, and it was the best job I ever had in my life. It was marvelous. I had 30 people who worked for me. I had a 14 million-dollar budget that I controlled. It wasn't without its pressures, trials, and tribulations, but it was wonderful.

Retirement was very difficult. I was miserable. I missed my job, I missed the people. It was a huge adjustment. But I've gotten to—it's almost good now. I joined the W.I.S.E. [Worcester Institute for Senior Education] Program. I'm the treasurer of it now. And I'm on the board of AdCare Hospital, which is a substance abuse hospital in Worcester. I've been on that board since 1994. I'm on the International Tourism Board that meets from time to time. I joined the J.C.C. [Jewish Community Center] and I take care of grandchildren, which is great. It was a huge adjustment, and I don't recommend it. Keep working, keep the mind going.

Barbara Haller
Age 58
Interviewed on October 27, 2005 by Justine Lambert of Worcester State University

So the City Manager put together this group called the City Manager's Advisory on Beacon-Brightly, and I was recruited to join it as a business owner on Main Street. It was right up my alley. I realized the neighborhood was the biggest deterrent to my business [Gilrein's, a live music club specializing in blues, jazz, and rock] being successful. These people didn't want to come to the neighborhood because it was too scary. So I joined and formed lot of friendships and allegiances with people, including Janice Nadeau, the City Councilor who represented the neighborhood. She [Nadeau] got sick during the campaign of 2001, and started to step down, and asked me to take her place. So that's how I got started in politics.

I was not a politician. I was the underdog in the election, but won. I had a resounding victory. So I got on the Council, but I didn't have the experience of the Council. I didn't know how city government was organized. And one of the writers for *Worcester Magazine* wrote, "It's going to be interesting to see if Barbara can make the transitions from activist to politician." And I remember being outraged...but I did find out that she was right...Being a politician was very different from being an activist. And learning all the protocols and the seniorities and who to get what done and who you have to mention and how thin-skinned people are—it makes my head spin.

I've tried to use my role as City Councilor to make government more accessible to neighborhoods. We have a lot of poverty and we have a lot of immigrant people who don't understand the culture, who don't understand how to make their way in Worcester. We have a lot of people who want to start their own businesses that don't quite know how to do it. And so, if I can link people to what they need to gain access to, to make things go forward, then that's the role that I've tried to play. And I also feel that if we listen to our neighborhoods, we'll know where to put our priorities in a large measure. So if you meet with neighborhoods and they talk about public safety—there's a drug house down the street or there's a gang of kids hanging around—then we know we need to bring public resources to that. So more than a top down, I'm more of a bottom up person.

We have more problems than any other district, in my district. We have the highest immigration; highest mobility, people moving around; lowest education; highest number of social services; number of single households; highest crime levels; worst streets and sidewalks; lowest income. The median income for a family of four is

$45,000—my district is $18,000. Large Hispanic population, but increasingly Southeast Asian, African, Albanian, and Eastern European all are common.

I feel like we have come a long way. We've made progress as females, but I would say now we have to make progress with our non-English speaking diversity. But we fail dismally in terms of integrating people…There's huge barriers to that, and discrimination and prejudice are two of the huge barriers. We can solve a lot of these problems. We have to stay at the table. We've got to leave our egos somewhat at the door, and just keep battering our way…I feel like I've played a small role in that because I'm female and because of my experience in American society.

Melanie Demarais
Age 51
Interviewed on April 2, 2008
by Maggie Dion and Danielle Defosse of Assumption College

I'm currently the President of the League of Women Voters in Worcester. The League was created in 1920 after women got the right to vote…It was an organization developed to create information at the [grassroots] level for all citizens, male and female. We didn't have TV or internet back then…This organization throughout the country gave people the opportunity to be informed citizens. So that when they go to the polls, they are informed. So nationally we take a lot of positions on a variety of topics, whether it's healthcare, the environment, politics, and whatever. We are a non-partisan group which means we don't favor either party, we try to educate all citizens to the issues that are out there…We are known for our unbiased and fair approach so that people feel when they go to a League [of Women] Voters program, there is no hidden agenda.

I joined the League four years ago, and clearly it's a group of mature women who have been active in this group for 30 to 40 years. And they really want to bring in a group of younger women to get involved and continue, carry on the legacy...I went to the National Convention two years ago...Our League just had a study on immigration, ...so the National League put aside money to have a study group put together. All of the issues and questions regarding immigration, whether it be students or the elderly...the borders, do we put a wall up around the United States or do we not? All of these issues, they studied it and we put our local League together and we reviewed it. And we sent back our answers in terms of...what our consensus was...So every League, like thousands and thousands across the country are doing the same thing, sending in information up to the national [level]. So literally when we give a national position, the women from Worcester are represented as well as the women from Des Moines, Iowa.

I think this is really fabulous. There are not many grassroots programs out there, so it's neat to be a part of that and see how it plays out. So this summer at the convention they will share what this consensus is and what the National League will be sending to Washington to say the League of Women voters has studied this...issue, and this is the position we are taking.

I definitely want to focus our energy with getting younger women involved in it. ...The internet is the key to do it...Last summer we got called by [College of the] Holy Cross. They were setting aside work study funds to have a student coordinate a voter registration drive at Holy Cross. So they asked if...the League would supervise, so I said, "Yes." We had another student that's helping us with another project called *All about Worcester*. Every League has a pamphlet or booklet for the citizens and new residents to the area to understand what's the political makeup of the area, how is this town organized or this city organized. She's helping us to update it...I have another woman from Boston University who is a Journalism major and she is minoring in Women's Studies...She is working with us on a couple of projects.

The world only goes around if you spin it...Your life is so much more rich and fulfilling if you choose to join an organization, if you join a group. It's a church group, or whatever it might be, but be active in your life 'cause you will have a much more full and rich life because you are giving your talent and gift to other people. And then you receive in the end.

And vote!...I have always voted. To me...I would take the day off to go vote, it's so important to me...We shouldn't put up so many barriers, I believe we want people to vote. We want them to be informed, but we want them to vote. So I feel bad that more people don't take it seriously. It's our greatest right as a citizen.

Lee Norton Kelly
Age 58
Interviewed on October 21, 2005 by Emily Bomba of Worcester State University

My husband is an oral surgeon and he decided to practice in Worcester. Almost 30 years ago we moved here from Boston lock, stock, and barrel. I was a teacher. I also worked in an all-women's high school for 15 years in a fundraising capacity. I am now the managing director of a not-for-profit that covers the entire New England area. I have also been very involved in volunteerism.

I currently sit on two non-profit boards. For many years I was very involved with the Junior League of

Worcester. The Junior League is an organization of women that promotes volunteerism in the community. I was on the executive committee and I chaired a couple of their fundraising events. For a number of years their major fundraiser was the Decorator's Showhouse. The League would contact an individual and offer to have professionals redecorate her home. The professionals volunteered their time and effort. A fee was then charged for folks to come in and see the magnificent structure and the beautiful furnishings. I worked on three of those. For one, I was the chair and I was in charge of making sure it all happened. It took a lot of work and a lot of hours, but it was so worth it. It was so wonderful. All of the monies that were raised were put right back into community projects which benefited the city.

I was also involved with the Dental Auxiliary. We would go into schools and give presentations about good dental health. We talked about how to brush your teeth and how often you should visit the dentist. It was done with little children. If you train little children, they will hopefully carry that knowledge and information and skill on. We had a character named Brushy Beagle that was essentially a person in a large dog costume. She would come into the classroom waving this huge toothbrush, and the kids thought it was so cool. It was really fun and a great way to reach children.

My husband and I became the primary caretakers for both of our mothers. This is a form of volunteering, though not in a structured way. While this may not have been in a formal and organized setting, it was very rewarding and enabled us to give back to the parents who gave us so much. It was a wonderful experience for us, sometimes very draining and very exhausting, but it was the kind of thing we felt very strongly had to be done.

I have also been involved with the American Association of University Women. I was also involved with the Audio Journal, which is a radio reading service for people who are visually impaired. I've worn a lot of hats. I think that has to do with wanting to give back to the community. The community of Worcester is very important. By being a part of various organizations I hopefully accomplished some things that benefited the city and its residents. I enjoy working with people, so it all just seemed a natural fit.

Mary Lou Anderson
Interviewed on March 23, 2009 by Arielle Ortiz of Assumption College

My family was very involved in politics...There were three girls. We were treated very well and we were taught to stand up for ourselves. It was a kind of household where my father questioned authority, so that probably fell more on me to question it.

I always wanted to be a teacher... I was teaching English in 1968-1969 at Burncoat Senior High and there was...this division of labor...If you wanted to show a film, you always had the boys go to the media center room and get the projector. If you had anything involving even light physical labor, it was automatically the boy. And the girls would deliver a note or something like that. And I began to think in my own head that there was something wrong with this...So I would have a girl go and do it [get the projector]. The girls didn't say, "Oh, I can't do that because I'm a girl." They would go and do it.

Worcester has a City Manager form of government. The City Manager runs the city...So a group of us women who met regularly called ourselves the Worcester Women's Network. We got the City Manager to create a commission called the City Manager's Advisory Commission on Women. And I was part of that. I was the Vice-Chair on that committee.

I've never missed an election in my entire life. I vote in presidential primaries, I vote in all primaries. I'm a member of the Democratic Party and I go to the caucuses. I've been to Democratic Conventions. [My husband] was an American History professor at [College of the] Holy Cross for many years. He was also in politics. He was a member of the Worcester City Council for 22 years and the mayor of the city of Worcester. So I've always been involved in politics and my uncle was the mayor of Worcester. [James O'Brien]

At the same time that I was teaching high school, I also taught a course or two at Assumption College...I ended up resigning from the public schools... And then I went back to school to get my Doctorate and...an opportunity made itself available at Assumption. President Joe Hagan...asked me if I would be interested in being the Acting Dean of Graduate and Continuing Education...I said, "Yeah, I'd like to do that under one condition, that I can be a candidate for that job." So, I finished my Doctorate and I did the job, and became a candidate, and got the job.

You end up choosing your battles on things. My husband and I are practicing Catholics. We go to the same parish in the city and at our parish during Lent, they decided to have a luncheon every Tuesday and a speaker on something in regard to Catholicism. Alright now, my husband retired. He still teaches a course at Holy Cross...so one of the priests of the church asked him if he would give a talk at one of the luncheons...Now I'm the Dean of a college, a Catholic college. I wasn't asked to do it. And then they asked my husband to do it again because people like him...But when he said, "No, I can't do it again, I'm doing something else," and it never dawned on them, "Well we could ask his wife. You know, she's the Dean of a college." I do think it's indicative of things. That's a minor thing. In the scheme of things it's minor. But I think...there are just little slights out there and there still are preferences given to men on some issues.

I think many things have changed in our society, so that there are more opportunities for young women and for people of other ethnic and racial backgrounds…But they haven't changed so much that obstacles aren't there. In my own experience, sometimes somebody will automatically think to ask a man before a woman. And that still exists.

You also always have to be aware that when you come into any kind of a position, you have to double-check that the man is not being paid more than you are being paid, and there are all kinds of ways of getting around that. You now see more women going to law school, more women going to medical school. But notice when they go to medical school, what fields they go into. They become pediatricians, or they go into internal medicine. You don't see many women going into surgery.

I think as women we do listen a bit more, and I think we also are probably more understanding and are more compassionate. Now I think that has to do more with how we're raised and environment…So is a woman's style different from a man's style? Are we more willing to give somebody a chance? There are all kinds of debates about that.

My advice would be to decide what you want to do and then pursue that, and don't let anything stop you. You should be confident enough that you can do what you want to do. I think I [had] an advantage being in administration and management. I've always thought one advantage I had is that I grew up in a very feisty political family. So, I tend to think politically, and I think that can be helpful.

Virginia Swain
Age 64
Interviewed on October 28, 2007
by Cara Joyce of the College of the
Holy Cross

I spent two years as a Peace Corps volunteer, and that completely changed my life. I was educated to think that the United States was the center of the world. All of a sudden I was in Africa, in Liberia, and I realized we weren't the center of the world. And that was a rude awakening for me. They taught us that we were supposed to tell people what to do, and I knew that was wrong. I decided to learn from the African people and have it be more mutual, like a citizens-exchange.

I traveled all over Africa in a way that totally opened my eyes to other ways of doing things, other ways of being. I was like a sponge. I was incredibly open to learning. So I learned how people can live together, very different, and support each other. They don't step over the poor the way we do. They just invite them into their homes. And it was such a shock to see, in a nice way.

Going back to the chronology of my life, I became an HR [Human Resources] Manager for Pepperidge Farms, which is a division of Campbell Soup. My brother called me one day to say that he was very upset and could I have lunch with him. And right at that moment my boss came in, and said he needed to see me right away. It was lunchtime and I couldn't manage both. So I put my brother off and said can we do it another day. The next day I got a call from my mother, and she said that my brother had been killed in a car accident.

This was a very formative experience for me because I was putting my career over my family, and my priorities were all mixed up. I ended up leaving the corporate world. I didn't think my values could be consistent with the values of the corporate world. I really felt something shift in me. My father died and my first marriage ended. I was really quite low. I started to realize that I needed to get off the treadmill. So I took a sabbatical and moved to California for 18 months. I went through training to become a spiritual director. I think this was the most creative time in my life.

I was contacted by Bernie Siegel, a very famous doctor who wrote *Love, Medicine, and Miracles*. He worked with cancer patients who learned a lot about the power of forgiveness in their lives, and how they could improve the quality of their lives, even if they lived for just a little bit longer. This was a consulting opportunity for me that combined my spiritual direction practice and my HR experience. It was really interesting because I was helping people glorify their values and helping organizations move through stress and conflict.

In the early 1990s the U.N. [United Nations] passed the Persian Gulf Resolution to stop Iraq invading Kuwait. I just knew at the core of my being that resolution was wrong. So I got on a train and went to the U.N. I feel that when you get in touch with your purpose and vision, all the doors are open for you. I have now worked for the U.N. for 18 years.

I learned a lot about how to innovate in a large system with something very positive and create change. I have two institutions that I started, the Institute for Global Leadership and the Center for Global Community and World Law, which I co-founded with my husband. I stand for a new way of looking at things. I've worked on five continents now. I have a deep respect for the way others operate and a deep respect for supporting them to find their own interests. I tend to focus on the proactive rather than the reactive.

I'm starting a new initiative here in Worcester called the Culture of Peace Initiative. I've been working with it at the U.N. for a number of years. It's going to be a three-year project where we'll invite Worcester individuals, groups, and coalitions to collaborate differently and work together for a common goal. I'm hoping to develop a template for the Worcester project that could go from city to city. We would focus on respect, solidarity, tolerance, and the environment.

Peace begins with respect. I've been developing leadership programs in reflective leadership and reconciliation leadership. I started a Global Mediation and Reconciliation Service where I've been working conferences around the world, helping refugees from Rwanda, Yugoslavia, and all the African countries, who are having such a hard time acclimating in this country. My whole project has been to develop community among those people who feel a sense of mission, that they want to make a difference but they don't know how to form a community of support.

Our job is to wake up to what is possible and to be conscious of our unconscious. I take a lot of solace in that even though I'm more awake than I was a few years ago, I'm still waking up. I believe in the collaboration and that balance between teaching and learning. So because of all my journeys, and because I have expertise and because I have understanding of what being a global citizen is in my own city, I feel that I can make a contribution.

Elizabeth Dean
Age 79
Interviewed on October 19, 2007 by Meghan Lytle of Worcester State University

I had an interesting job along with all the other recent college graduates at the Institute of International Education in New York. We were evaluating applications for grants. They came from different countries around the world, so it was very interesting to learn about different colleges they were interested in and around the United States. I first learned about Worcester when I realized they were applying to some of the local colleges and the reasons and the departments and so forth that they felt were worthwhile. So it was a very interesting responsibility.

The first thing I did after I was married and came to Worcester, was to become involved in the League of Women Voters. My mother had been involved in the League of Women Voters back in Duluth, Minnesota, and I met a wonderful group of people. It really took up a great deal of my time for those first years. We had all sorts of programs and it was very different then. That is one of the real changes today because we were at-home mothers for the most part, and not too many were working. It was when we were just starting to go to work, so we had day-time meetings and we studied areas of the world in terms of international relations. We worked on all sorts of things.

At that time there were enough women available so we could have meetings and really study issues. We had three meetings, for example, studying a particular issue and then we would present it to the whole organization for a consensus. Then we went into it versus the state and then the nation. It was much more of a grassroots organization that it can be now because so many women are working. It's very hard, working women will arrange meetings for Saturday mornings or evenings, but it's sometimes hard for them to do it all. It's not the same, but it's still a wonderful organization. I admire it tremendously and support it. But it doesn't give you the chance to come together with people on a regular basis and get to know people. That was so wonderful for me.

If there was something to do with treaties, we would study the areas of the world involved in the treaties. Of course, we are big supporters of people working together internationally. Everyone reported on what she had discovered and learned and then we came to consensus. It was just an incredible learning experience but then little by little I got more into things internationally.

Early on I became involved in the International Centre. We had a marvelous program for newcomers to the community. The Worcester Foundation for Experimental Biology had many doctors and we got to know the wives and had English programs for them. We had a regular English language program for them to help because they came from all around the world. Then our home for hospitality was wonderful. In those days, I think, again it had a lot to do with women at home and the kinds of people who came. But we tried to match people who wanted to invite people to their homes with the people in what part of the world they might be interested in. It was fascinating. I worked as a volunteer and then I became Coordinating Director. I felt as if the world was a wonderful place and we could do something to help those who came from around the world.

I am working a bit with Preservation Worcester. I am a docent of sorts, guiding tours and so forth downtown. I used to go to the schools and talk to third graders about the meaning of architecture, what it was like in their neighborhood and we would take little walks in their neighborhoods. We tried to get them excited about their own neighborhoods, for example, "This is what is here, this is special, isn't this great, etc." It's all part of the learning process.

Well I try to keep informed and I guess politics is my major thing. I'm working now with the city with the Green Hill Park Coalition. If you come up over the hill on Belmont Street, there is a drive called Skyline Drive and when you go off, there's a park that was given to the city over 100 years ago. It had been pretty much neglected. They got the city to be determined to go ahead with it and they did a wonderful job of bringing it up to date and making it beautiful. But then they wanted to build a school on park property. The Worcester Technical High School, the new high school here is a gorgeous high school, but we fought them about building it on park property. In the end, the city did build a school there. But we do have what they call 'continuing responsibilities,' in other words, there are certain things that the city cannot do in the park without consulting us. There is also the idea that if they had a school there, the students have to take educational programs on the environment and give so many hours a year to managing the park. That's something we try to keep very close track of.

Thea Aschkenase
Age 86
Interviewed on February 20, 2009 by Johanie Rodriguez of Worcester State University

I was born a Jewish child in Germany, and I was a happy child until Hitler came to power. At our apartment house we had a big yard, and children congregated there to play. All of a sudden, kids did not want to play with my brother and me. We didn't do anything, we didn't have a fight. Now I think their parents told them not to play with Jewish kids. Around the time I was 14, we couldn't go to movies or parks, and we were sent away from public schools. They made a Jewish school for all the Jewish kids in Munich. A father of one of my friends jumped out a window and killed himself. They said that he was too friendly to German women. It was the fact that any accusation against a Jew was taken for granted.

In 1938 we were told that we had to leave Germany or be sent to a concentration camp. There seemed to be no place in the world that would give us permission to enter. We were desperate. All of a sudden, Italy opened the borders and said, "No questions asked, just cross the border and come." I'm forever grateful for the Italian people that they did this for us.

In Munich we had a big apartment. In Italy we had one room for my father, my mother, my brother, and myself. A year later the Italian government made an alliance with the Germans, and they had to send all the foreign men to a concentration camp. The women and children were sent to a different place until they decided what they would do. Then they sent us to the camp my father was in. It was a good camp. You had food. There was a playing field, and we founded a kindergarten for the children. Everybody was extremely tolerant and friendly.

After a year it was decided that the families should go out to different villages. We were sent to Villanova D'asti. We stayed there a year and a half. The people were wonderful to us. It was a wonderful place to wait for the end of the war. We hoped that we could go back to Germany at the end of the war. The young Italian girls made some trips to a nearby movie with bicycles. I always went with them and was lent a bicycle.

Then in 1943 or '44 our landlady told us the Germans were coming. This wonderful, wonderful lady took us to a hiding place in the north of Italy in the mountains. Somebody gave us their barn, and we slept on straw. Some others gave us blankets. My mother and father found work in the village. One day, a boy who was staying with us in the barn, was chased by Italian soldiers. The soldiers were looking for freedom fighters. Harry led them back to the barn, and the soldiers discovered that we were Jewish. They took us to a prison in Turino. The men and women were divided into separate areas. The Germans took over, and we remained there for two months. Then we were told that we were being sent to a labor camp. We were overjoyed. That means we were going to be together with my father and brother.

We were taken to the railroad station, and the Germans were there. We were put into cattle cars, the big ones where they transport animals. It was very scary. After five days, the train stopped and it said Auschwitz. There was a sign, "Arbeit Macht Frei, Work Makes Free," by which one assumes it's a working camp. But it wasn't. When we marched into Auschwitz, there was the infamous Dr. Mengele. He did experiments on people. He selected the people who entered Auschwitz, and who would live and who would die. So we entered, my father, my brother, my mother, and I with no idea what was going to happen. Dr. Mengele put me in one group and my father and mother in another group. But I grabbed my mother and put her back to my side. Dr. Mengele said to my mother, "I have put you in the other group." God forbid you don't speak to a German in any of those camps, but I said, "No, no I have seen you put her there." I don't know why he let me get away with it, maybe because I spoke German. He let my mother stay with me and this saved her life.

So we were sent to take a shower and all the German men were there making comments. It was very humiliating. I wondered to what camp they had sent my father. One of the women took me outside, and there was a big building and smoking chimney. She said, "He went up in smoke already." Old people and children and the mothers that didn't want to let go of their children were all killed within the hour they came into Auschwitz.

The hunger was terrible there. We had one piece of bread in the morning and some watery soup at noontime. The bread had to last until the next morning. Some people ate it right away, and most of us hid it on our body. My mother got very sick and every week or two there was a selection of Germans who came to the barracks and made us all undress. They selected the people who were not healthy anymore.

We were there maybe ten months. From there we were sent to a labor camp. The labor camp was better. Then one morning the Germans had disappeared, and soldiers were marching to camp. We found out it was the Russians. They said the war was over. The Germans had surrendered unconditionally in Europe. We didn't know where we were and they said, "You can go to the nearby village and look for food." So we went there and didn't find food. The Germans had taken all the food.

My mother and I left the second day to walk back to Italy. Now we were in upper Germany. We were on the road for four months. We hitchhiked, that was the mode of transportation. We had some money from a relief organization that I kept in my shoe. With the money we rode some trains. But the trains were dangerous because Russians came in and took some of the girls to their compartment. They made them drunk, forced them to drink, and raped them.

We came back to Milano. We stayed a few months, but we heard that all of our relatives had been killed. So the Jewish Brigade found a ship that transported people to Palestine. We stayed in Israel for seven to eight years. I married and had a daughter there. It was really wonderful. In 1954, we came to the United States. We moved to Brooklyn and then my husband found a job in Clinton, Massachusetts. I said that Clinton was too small for me, so we moved to Worcester.

I had a son here. European men don't like their wives to work, so when I came here I stayed home. When my son went to college, I said, "I want to go to work." I worked at UMass Medical [University of Massachusetts Medical Hospital] for 15 years as an aide in therapy. Then I said, "Now I am going to school." I went to Worcester State [Worcester State University]. I was terrified to go to school. After ten years, I graduated.

No matter what, family is your strongest ally. Even if you dislike someone, just be close to the family because it's a terrible thing if you lose the whole family. The main thing is, don't judge other people because they have a different language, a different opinion, or a different skin color. They wanted me to come back to Germany to talk to the German young people. I wanted to tell them just be tolerant because it's inconceivable that because somebody is Jewish or speaks a different language that they should be your enemy. Unfortunately, it takes a long time for people to accept that.

CHAPTER SIX

UNIQUELY WORCESTER REMEMBRANCES

"That motley mingling of abolitionists, socialists, and infidels, of all sexes and colors, called the Women's Rights Convention, assembled in this city, to-day, and an account of their proceedings we have the honor herewith to communicate to the New York Herald."

New York Herald, October 25, 1850

As mentioned in the introduction, Worcester was a leader in social, political, cultural, and economic change and a natural selection for the 1850 convention's site. Worcester was easily accessible by road, railroads, and the Blackstone Canal and its skilled workforce and large number of manufacturing companies made it an industrial center second only to Boston in the Commonwealth of Massachusetts. The leading speakers of the day including Frederick Douglass, Sojourner Truth, Harriet Tubman, and Wendell Phillips often travelled to Worcester to speak and its residents included Abby Kelley Foster, Steven S. Foster,

Isaiah Thomas, and also Lucy Stone and Clara Barton from the nearby towns of West Brookfield and Oxford.

The First National Woman's Rights Convention was only one of the things that can be called a Worcester "first." The cotton gin (1793), manufactured Valentine's Day cards (1847), liquid fuel rockets (1914), oral contraceptives (1960), and the Smiley Face (1964) were also born in Worcester or its suburbs.

Today, Worcester is the second largest city in New England and it is still rich in cultural and educational life. It is home to 13 colleges and universities and multiple museums and libraries including Higgins Armory, Worcester Historical Museum, American Antiquarian Society, Worcester Art Museum, and EcoTarium. It is also home to a thriving medical community and developing biotechnology industry.

So many of the women who were interviewed for the Worcester Women's Oral History Project spoke of memories of Worcester and their feelings for their hometown that this additional chapter is included to capture some of these uniquely Worcester experiences. This chapter reveals some of Worcester's historical events, its treasures, and also concerns for future growth and development. It shares recollections of trolleys in the downtown area and the disruption of neighborhoods caused by the building of Interstate 290 as well as appreciation of the three-deckers and Victorian architecture in various parts of the city.

Two tragic events that are a part of Worcester's history are seared in the memories of more than a few of the women. The Tornado of 1953 was the most severe tornado in New England history and resulted in 94 deaths, 1,300 injuries, and 15,000 homeless and whether they were younger or older at the time, many women mentioned where they were when it struck and how it affected them or their neighbors. A more recent tragedy occurred when six firefighters were killed in the Worcester Cold Storage Fire of

1999. The memorial service was nationally broadcast and attended by President Bill Clinton, Vice President Al Gore, and Senators Edward M. Kennedy and John F. Kerry. Although these two events put Worcester in the national headlines, the following stories are examples of individuals' feelings of pride in a hometown that is a city of neighborhoods and diversity. Or as one woman describes Worcester, "it is more of a stew than a soup."

Frances Gertrude Levine
Age 103
Pictured on her 100th birthday
Interviewed on April 4, 2007 by
Judy Freedman Fask

[I was born on] January 12, 1904 in Pinsk/Minsk. [I was] not born here, but grew up here....in a Jewish neighborhood—Water Street, Harrison, Fox Street and all those streets. My father worked for a contractor who was offered work in Worcester....so we moved to Worcester. [He] worked as a piece maker, as a pants maker....and for a few pennies more when they offered him a job in Worcester, he accepted. But he would not open any business on his own; he would not leave his ties with the union. That meant more to him than anything else....and as much as my mother could use him at home, when Saturday came he was busy, he had to go to sick people at the hospital. What else can I remember? He was very active and very handsome. I remember her [my mother] making—rolling the dough and making the challah, and making the little—she'd smear them with eggs and put them in the oven.

All the kids were in one bed, my mother had her own. There was an upstairs and a downstairs, and I slept in the alcove of the downstairs, that was my bedroom. I had an egg box that was my bureau…..The bottom part I kept a couple of pair of pants, and on the top a couple of tops and then I had two middy blouses, one I wore and one I had to wash and had to wait to dry so I could wear to school the next day. In the summertime there was no hot water, but in the wintertime they had a coal-burning stove so there was hot water. Food was no problem; we always had enough food, because for very little money they could fix all those variety dishes. And the boys always had the best pants, knickers, we used to wear knickers. The girls were the first girls to wear long pants to school. Because their daddy made them, your grandfather.

I must have been 17, but I worked for a couple of years for my high school clothes. I worked in a store for a lady. She told my mother that she knew that I was very honest. They deliberately left things around. I always put them back where they belonged. She couldn't understand that I could be so honest as a big family like that. I was [also] selling excess merchandise from the First World War and I would get $1.00 for one hundred envelopes. So I was addressing envelopes. [I liked to] read, go to the movies. My mother would give me ten cents. A nickel for the movie and a nickel for candy. [My favorite movie was] *The Perils of Pauline*.

You know when we came to Worcester from South Norwalk, it was just prior to the flu epidemic [of 1918]. Now mama had to go to the hospital with Eli. Papa and I stayed home with one of the boys—we were the survivors—and mama had to drag Eli, who was a big boy. None of the kids had any of the childhood diseases …….until Barbara went to public school. That's when she got the measles and the chicken pox and the mumps. I didn't have anything.

Margery Dearborn
Age 82
Interviewed on November 21, 2006 by Alyssa Bell of Worcester State University

I first married James Donnelly who was a native of Worcester. He died in 1971. Then I married Otto Vincent Gustafson, also a native of Worcester and he died in 1989. And then I married Richard Wright Dearborn, who was a native of Cape Elizabeth, Maine, a lawyer in the city of Worcester. And I'm still married to him.

I lived in Newton for a number of years and moved to Worcester with my husband in 1952. I've been here ever since! It was a big adjustment, but once I grew to like the city, I grew to love the city. I don't want to live anywhere else! [My neighborhood was] big, old Victorian houses on a fairly wide street. Well, similar a little to the Westland, Germaine, and Haviland Street areas of Highland Street here in Worcester. But the yards were larger, we had more land between the houses.

Generally, I think that the city is great. I don't think it's as attractive a city as it could be or should be, and many years ago I helped found Preservation Worcester because it was, you know, it seemed important to me. The impetus was the three Greek Revival houses at the bottom of Lincoln Street, right near Lincoln Square, and they were being demolished to make way for a supermarket and a parking lot. And one of them was a house where [Charles] Dickens stayed when he visited the city in the 1850s. They were quite wonderful buildings and the city was modernizing itself and we were beginning to lose the buildings that gave the city its flavor – that made Worcester its own city rather than a carbon copy of everything else.

The destruction of the 19th century buildings and the erection of the 20th century Worcester Centrum in 1970 was perhaps the biggest change downtown. Before that, downtown was a crowded area everyday—especially on Saturdays. The stores were open and vital and there was just a whole lot of activity going on downtown. There isn't that anymore and I'd like to see it come back.

Dolores Courtemanche
Age 73
Interviewed on November 12, 2008 by Gina Casadonte and Nicole Macioci of Assumption College

I had been working as a waitress and, you know, that was such a menial job back then. Then all of sudden I'm working for a newspaper and I'm a reporter. And it was like. "Where did she come from?"—you know people that knew me. But I read constantly. I remember once working as a cashier in this restaurant and I was reading. It was a very, very slow winter night, and some state trooper walked in and said, "Reading a dirty book?" And those kinds of—this made me crazy. And I just held up the book and it was the end of the conservation. The book happened to be the autobiography of Benjamin Franklin. I could have been reading *Hawaii* or something else like that, but anyway he just went and sat down. On his way out he stopped and apologized. And so, anyway, I read a lot. And so when I got the job it was because of my tests were, were very high. But I found it very interesting because all of a sudden I was a different person in some people's eyes. You know, especially in a small town. All of a sudden I'm a reporter and people, you know, inviting me places or just, you know, they know me and it was, that was a little bizarre. But then I was at the paper so many years and that's more my, my persona now, so I don't even think about it.

I learned an awful lot on the job. It was a learning experience for 25 years. I was a reporter for the *Worcester Telegram*. It was better than working. [Laughs] It was—it was *very* interesting. It was like a liberal arts education, because I did feature stories that could range from medical stories at UMass [University of Massachusetts Medical School], to interviewing all sorts of people...people from real life or... some celebrities that came in or out of Worcester or wrote books...and well known people in the Worcester area about what was going on. So it was never the same.

I think it was a week before I retired, the [December 3, 1999 Worcester Cold Storage] Fire that killed all those fireman. We had a big, big memorial service, with fireman from all over the country—I think some from Europe. And President [Bill] Clinton was here, and that was very, very moving and touching. It did have some impact. I think it— once again, it made Worcester seem like a small community and not a city.

A retarded woman was living in an abandoned factory down by—there was a diner, right where you go to get onto Grafton Street, around that area. Anyway, she was living with some guy and they had candles. And that's how the fire started. And then, she was afraid, so they ran away and the fire took and it was—just was a *big blaze*, and we lost, I think, seven [post-interview correction: six] firefighters.

It was very, very tragic. And she was—it was pathetic, she was mentally retarded [and] she had a twin sister who had been adopted—she hadn't. And the twin sister lived in New Hampshire and had a very nice family, and they took this girl in, and she had to go to trial. She got off because of you, know, all these extenuating circumstances, and she's living in New Hampshire and has a little job, and doing very well.

Theresa O'Neill
Age 73
Interviewed on November 13, 2006 by Shawn O'Neill of Worcester State University

I was born during the Depression so when we were kids we were kind of on the poor side. We had a neighborhood movie and you could go almost anytime—mostly I went on a Saturday. But my girlfriend's mother—they used to give out dishes on Tuesday night and my girlfriend's mother wanted two of everything. So she would pay my way to the movies on ... Tuesday night. And I would get to see for free whatever was playing. Twelve cents [was the price of movies]. Twenty-nine cents a gallon of gasoline. My first job paid 60 cents an hour.

It was nice [the Greendale neighborhood]. Everybody knew everybody. And we had the fairgrounds right next to our house so there was a million things to do over there. When the circus was coming to town, we'd get to sleep on the front porch so we could hear them coming in. And Indian Lake we had at the top of the hill. We played. We didn't have a lot of toys – we played with Mother Nature.

We had a bus, but that was a dime and a lot of times you didn't have a dime. So we'd walk downtown which was probably five or six miles I'd say. And on a Saturday morning, Saturday and Sunday morning, we'd walk to church.

Dates are different now. I can remember one time, I was going out with this fella and—I never asked my parents how old I had to be to start dating. I was 14 and he walked up to my neighborhood and we went for a walk and where we walked was the route my father came home from work. And he saw us, but he never said anything about it so I guess it was alright. I think I was 16 when I started dating and going to the movies or something. And most of the boys didn't have cars and you met downtown. Once in a blue moon, a guy would take a trip to your house and then you would go back on the same bus downtown. Mostly you walked a lot.

I lived up at the Summit then [1953 Tornado] which was still Greendale. We didn't get hit, but I was on my way home from work and saw all these cars coming toward us that were all covered in mud and dust. Somebody said a train went off the tracks at the Summit ... and then I get up to Assumption College and there was a guy sitting like up against a tree trunk and he had no head and I was so scared. Then my kid brother came home. By then we knew it was a tornado. Then, of course, someone started a rumor that it was coming back. So I take my—and my kid sister came home—and I took those two down cellar just because I thought it would be safe there. So that was a terrible thing. You just had never seen anything like that before. The worst part was now half of Assumption College got knocked right off and the top floor. I don't think it took them too long to rebuild—probably a year.

Barbara Murphy
Interviewed on October 20, 2006 by Laura Murphy of Worcester State University

We both [she and her best friend Connie] got jobs in the telephone company and we thought we were millionaires because the telephone company was really the place that really paid women then. I was an information operator. It was great. It was all women. That was a great place to work. You know, they taught you everything first and then they put you on different things. It was great to have all women. That's what I think of on my whole life, that how great it was to have all women—working women—women teach you to do everything. It's a whole different ball game with that. You know, women could rule the world [Laughs]

I was married April 23, 1949 at St. Peter's. And my sister, Patsy, was my bridesmaid and Connie was my maid of honor. And Miss Claire was the organist and in those days you could tell her what you wanted and she played all the music I wanted. So it was great. I had a gown—and not everybody [had one]—and veil. We had our reception in the Crystal Room. It's 50 Franklin Street—it used to be the Bancroft Hotel. It was the nicest place and it was really [laughs]—in my mother's day they used to dance on the roof. And we went to New York for our honeymoon. And that was when Worcester first started having airplanes coming to the airport and we were one of the first ones. That was the first time I had ever been on an airplane.

When we were first married we lived on Pleasant Street. That was right after the war in a way—you know, World War II. And then after we were there for a while, they were building this great thing for Worcester. It was going to be the Curtis Apartments and they were going to be way out at the end of Lincoln Street and they were for the veterans that were coming home. And that turned into Great Brook Valley. And so we put in, and we went to live out there, way out there. Everything was perfect. Everyone that you knew [laughs] lived out there. It was the best thing. It was so much fun. And there wasn't a church out there that was the one thing. This is how things went in those days. And so we actually all contributed when we got out there and they built St. Joan of Arc Church.

Franny was born in February and the tornado was June 9th. He was a baby and I had Martha and Barbara. And the day of the tornado we were all out—all the people were out there in the park. And then all of a sudden it starts raining, and all of a sudden the wind starts blowing. We just all started taking our wash in and running in the house to get away. And then I was by myself with the three kids and I remember I was gonna make spaghetti for that night and the spaghetti was all over the kitchen when we went back to see it. It was mostly just women who were at home because the men hadn't come home from work. There was a guy and Clooney was his name. And he had just gotten home from work and he was saying, "Get down! Get down! Get down!" And he was telling us that we should go down to the basement. And we all went down to the cellar and we were there. And Dad [her husband] comes home and doesn't know it – nobody in the city knows it that we were all going [into the basements] 'cause it was so crazy. Nobody knows that the Curtis [Apartments] have been, you know, it was all battered down, lots of roofs were gone and everything. It was unbelievable when you came out of that cellar and saw what it really looked like up there. And he was coming home from work and he couldn't go any further than Lincoln Street. And he walked all the rest of the way home. And he came to the [Curtis Apartments] and saw that roofs were off some buildings. He was so worried to where we were, [laughs] but we were in the cellar. But then when he came, we just locked up the place, took some diapers—I can think of it now—and the milk that was in the refrigerator. And we walked up to where his car was and we got in and we went to my mother's house. [Laughs] But then when it was built again we went back there. It took them all summer to build it and repair it and everything, but we went back.

Zelda Schwartz
Age 71
Interviewed on November 9, 2010 by Daniel Johnson and Stephanie Plotkin of Assumption College

I lived in Worcester until 1957 when

I went away to college. And I came back to Worcester in 1970 when my husband opened his practice and went to work at the [UMass] Medical School. He became Assistant Professor in Medicine for the first medical school, class of 1970, and we've been here since—40 years.

Worcester was a small town when I was a little girl, and Main Street was vibrant. My mother didn't drive a car, so we took the trolley to "come down street," to go shopping down in—you just would not believe, but all of Main Street from down where Mechanics Hall is all the way to the end where the old Denholm Building is which was vibrant and Worcester Commons—Worcester Front Street was absolutely amazing. Culturally, I think it's exciting to live in Worcester, I think that the colleges here have a lot of intellectual stuff going on that we take advantage of. We're subscribers to Mechanics Hall, we're members of the [Worcester] Art Museum, we come to the film festival at Clark [University].

I'm a witness to the tornado that happened, the Worcester tornado that happened in – I'm trying to think when it was – [19]53. Anyways, '52 or '53, there was a terrible tornado. Have you heard about that? The story of the tornado? A tornado swept through the Greendale section …. and it took the lives of many, many people, terrible destructions. My husband and I were childhood sweethearts, and we were walking—he would walk me home and then I would walk him halfway home, and do all these things you do when you're 13 years old—and the sky got really, really black and he said, "You know what, I think you better go home your way, and I'm going my way." And it was about a quarter of four in the afternoon, and sometime within the next hour this tornado just blew through that section of Worcester, and we knew people who were in our religious school classes—the temple—who lived in different sections of the city—we grew up in a time we went to neighborhood schools, but we knew other kids from other neighborhoods from religious school, so we knew people who had passed away, who were in the Shrewsbury area. A classmate of ours went to close her window and the roof fell in. Anyways, the next day, obviously, it was a disaster area, school was closed, and we all went neighborhood to neighborhood collecting canned goods and clothing and taking them to some distribution centers just to help the people who had been so impacted. I think as a child that is probably the biggest thing that I do remember happening here.

Judith Jepson
Age 71
Interviewed on November 27, 2006 by Chris Jepson of Worcester State University

I used to do all of my shopping there [in Worcester], the wonderful department stores. I know we used to have a trolley that you could ride around in. It was a wonderful place to go and eat. Putnam and Thurston's was the greatest place to go to dinner. I remember [the factories] because my father worked at H.H. Brown for a couple of years, but most of those big, really big companies have left or have just died out. One thing [that makes Worcester distinct] is the three-deckers. I mean those are so—they are so unusual and I am very glad to see that they are being renovated and people are living in them again.

[During the World War II era] we moved from Maine where my father was a warden. We had to close down, make your house dark at night. We had tremendous rationing of food. We ate a lot of organ foods—beef tongue, liver, tripe—because those were available. We had oleo which was a white pack of some kind of fat and had a colored dye that you pushed, pushed on it and it turned this massive white whatever into a yellow whatever that barely tasted like anything. But we did it because the food was needed overseas for the men who were fighting.

My father went on to become an incredibly successful manufacturer and he started on literally a bootstrap and then started making boots. He bought John Frye's shoe company in Marlborough [Massachusetts] in 1945 I believe or '46 and kept building and building and building the business up until it became probably one of the most famous boot companies. Cowboy boots, boots for servicemen, and in the '70s and '80s it was—you had to have Frye boots or you didn't have the proper outfit on. My husband worked for Frye Boot Company in Marlborough and ended up being president of it before he retired.

Shirley Coleman
Age 69
Interviewed on October 19, 2005 by Jeannette Perry of Worcester State University

I have lived in this neighborhood for 41 years. Before that I lived for three years in the Indian Hill section of Worcester. Most of the people in that area were of Swedish descent. The neighborhood I now live in has changed over 41 years. When I first moved in most of the people had lived here for many years. Today the neighborhood has young people who move often. I really do not know my new neighbors. Many of them don't speak English well.

I think the strong points in Worcester are our great colleges, one of the best music halls in the United States, and a beautiful convention center that has attracted big names from all over the world. One big plus is that we are near Boston and we can drive there often.

When I first arrived [to Worcester from New Hampshire], I was intimidated by the amount of traffic and for six years I would not drive to the downtown area. I came with my future husband for a tour of the city and I remember him showing me Mechanics Hall. It was beautiful. He then took me to meet his family. I thought Worcester was very big. It was congested with houses very close to each other.

The biggest change I have seen is the increased building of homes. So many homes, apartments, and condominiums have sprung up over the years. When we first moved here on this street it was a dirt road and there were five cellar holes left there from the Tornado of 1953. This area was completely demolished by the storm.

I remember the tornado and how you could not drive into Worcester because all the roads were blocked. It is funny that we live now in a house that was blown down by the tornado. It was rebuilt in 1954. My husband Leo and I were part of the rescue crew that assisted victims of the tornado. Every time I hear a thunderstorm I get very nervous. I still have visions of people lying dead in the field across from Curtis Apartments known as the Poor Farm. Corn used to be grown there by the paupers of the city. The landmark silo that remained when Social Security was made available for all and there was no need for the farm was completely destroyed. The people of Worcester were caught unaware, but we rallied and reached out to help those in need in any way we could.

Carol Donnelly
Age 60
Interviewed on November 19, 2006 by Colleen O'Brien of Worcester State University

My father was an Irishman who was the son of immigrants…and he was the youngest of eight children and he was a pretty talented guy. He played semi-pro baseball and was a boy's soprano. He studied music in the early 20th century and was a wandering minstrel on a radio show at WTAG in the 1930s. And then he served in the army during World War II, and one of his jobs was to direct the army choir in London.

My mom was French-Canadian. Her family had immigrated to Nova Scotia…but then came to the United States about the same time as my father's family. She worked as a telephone operator and then married my dad just at the beginning of World War II. My mother still lives in Auburn and she is 95…I have cousins around and an enormous passel of in-laws because my husband's family was also a Worcester family and he has cousins who have cousins who have cousins, and they are all around. You can't miss them.

The city was a really…vital manufacturing area…until after World War II, and since then manufacturing jobs have left, so the economic vitality of the city has sort of dissipated. Even as late as 1984 when we moved back, there were still lots of Worcester businesses, really big companies, lots of Worcester banks. People in the community actually could talk to people who owned the businesses and ran the banks, so there were lots of things that you could get done. Now there really aren't. There are a couple of little Worcester banks. Norton Company doesn't belong to Norton Company anymore. Morgan Construction is the only Fortune 500 Company that is locally owned.

We [my husband and I] both care an awful lot about the community, so…we do a lot of volunteer work. You know, major volunteer work for the [Worcester] Art Museum, work for Preservation Worcester. I've been on the board of a little daycare center forever. I'm just turning over the presidency of the Worcester Center for Crafts. He's been on the board…of the American Antiquarian Society. You know, Worcester is looking for people to support the organizations…The Craft Center I'm connected with because my daughter is in art school and she did a huge number of art classes there, so this is payback for all they did.

You know, the Art Museum is to preserve and interpret 2,000 years of art, and the Art Museum is way cool because it really is a cultural institution. The American Antiquarian Society...it's like Noah's Ark; it has one or two of everything that was printed in the United States from day one until about 1870. It's just an amazing institution. The Craft Center's goal is to sustain crafts and keep people doing and working with them. [At] the Craft Center being President of the Board...that's planning and implementing the agenda of all the board meetings. It was organizing the committee structure... Non-profits in the city are having a terrible time financially, so it's fundraising and planning fundraising. That was a big job and I'm handing it over tomorrow night.

We do belong to the Shakespeare Club of Worcester which is the oldest Shakespeare Club in the entire country. It is 125 years old and there are probably 70 of us, and every two weeks we meet and we go through all of Shakespeare's works.

[Worcester] has wonderful cultural vitality. You can fall out of bed and go to three museums and Mechanics Hall and art and music, and there's so much wonderful culture richness. And it's a pretty small town. You still can...have a sense about who's around you, who is doing what. It is certainly still a community that is more of a stew than a soup. You can still feel the different culture threads.

Charlyne Dore
Age 60
Interviewed on November 7, 2006
by Catherine Dore
of Worcester State University

During my life, I lived the first 36 years in the Webster Square area of Worcester. It was made up of large families, all large families, and everything was done in groups. You know, we sat on the porch in groups, we sat on the street in groups, we played ball in groups. There was a corner down the end of the street where everybody went—we called it The Oval. It was just a big plot of grass and everybody just congregated there. It was very, very family and group oriented.

But the neighborhoods have changed. The downtown—they've added a lot of shopping areas—those things have changed. But basically there's still neighborhoods. I think they've integrated the neighborhoods. Before it was all the Polish living in one area, Italians living in another.

The challenge is to get people to…stay within their city and support the city. I think the challenge is to get people to be loyal and use the things the city's got. The city's got plenty of stuff. That airport is like a white elephant—nobody wants to use it. The downtown area was very nice, but nobody wanted to use it.

The mixture of cultures, and different people and everybody [are what makes Worcester distinct]. And I think there's a large college infiltration in Worcester too with all the big colleges there. You really get a diverse amount of people with nationalities and religions and everything, and I think it's great—it's great for any city.

The Tornado [of 1953] hit and ... and we had relatives that lived out in the Great Brook Valley and I can remember [going] out there and seeing it and thinking, "The houses, half the houses are gone!" They were cut in half, they were gone, and there were areas where there were just, there were not trees at all. It was like someone had gone in with a big shredder and just shredded all the trees. And I also knew the girl that lost her legs. She lived near us and she was trapped under a—I think it was a refrigerator. Anyhow, she lost her legs in the tornado. She was one of the people that was injured, and we knew her, she went to the high school with us after that. But it was scary, it was.

Angela Penny
Age 52
Interviewed on April 16, 2008 by Kate Cibotti and Kristina Powell of Assumption College

There have been quite a lot of changes, schools closing, reorganization of the schools. I attended North High School, which was on Salisbury Street, I'm not sure if you're familiar with the old school, it was on Salisbury Street, an old brick building, very beautiful. The kids were moved up to Harrington Way to a school that was built in the '70s, which is almost obsolete now. And we're gonna have to knock that down and make a new school. And just the health industry has become big business in Worcester. It was such an industrial producing area and now it's like it's a healthcare industry. It starts on Medical City and it goes right up Belmont Street to Memorial Hospital, to UMass [Memorial]. It's like almost a medical city.

I mean if you know the history [of Worcester], I think it was pretty progressive at its time. To have the First Woman's Rights Convention in Worcester in 1850, right down on Main Street. There were women from all over the country that attended. People took trains to get here for the event. So I think it [Worcester] certainly has a history of having women involved. I think having a woman mayor is wonderful!

[The reenactment] was held in 2000. It was the 150-year anniversary of the actual Woman's Rights Convention. It was a wonderful experience because the women of that time were very vocal about their opinions. They wanted the right to vote, they wanted representation in government, and they didn't want to pay taxes for something they didn't have any representation in, and they were able to voice their feelings about injustices that they felt which were, you know, not being able to vote, not having a say, and also they did not approve of the slavery issue, so that was something that they fought strongly for. It was quite an honor to be a part of it, it was. You know I learned so much about that time, the people that were involved, and knowing that it happened right here in Worcester made it that much more important. You know, I often wondered how that got about, how they got to the convention, how they managed to stay in those dresses.

I worked up at the Worcester Historical Museum, I was a receptionist there—and just a world of knowledge, they have collections that they share. I got to actually hold a Civil War diary. It came through the front door and I was able to do that. I mean I got to read what this soldier actually ate for dinner. So I've had quite a varied opportunity to be really up close with some of this stuff. Daguerreotypes, I've actually held in my hand. Early, early photographs. It's before photography they had daguerreotypes which were done on glass—a photograph that's on glass. The museum has quite a few. And sometimes when people donate things to the museum, they come right through the front door and there I am at the front desk.

Restaurants, oh boy, we go a lot of different places. We're everywhere—Shrewsbury Street, Dino's, we hit a lot of the—mostly everything on the East Side. But, I'm over here too, like I said, I love to come to Assumption. Oh boy, I love the library; I do a lot of family research, Worcester history, that's a good resource for that. My first date was here at Assumption College. I went to the basketball game, Serge DeBari was on the team in those days, it was 1970, so he was on the team and now he's the coach. So everything that goes around comes around. So that was my first date. It seemed like the biggest gym ever. You walked in, I mean I was 15, we didn't—I mean a college campus and a college gym, we never saw more of a back yard or a schoolyard and grammar school, I thought it was the biggest gym. There were people everywhere, it was so exciting. And it was an exciting time for the school and the team was really good in those days. The team is still good; I come to the games a lot. I love basketball. I kind of forgot until I took my daughter to a game again, she wanted to go watch, so I took her, and I thought, "Wow, I remember how much fun this was, why don't I do this more often?" So I found myself at quite a few games.

I like to go to the [American] Antiquarian [Society] and hear the lectures they have over there. I love Elm Park. I love to walk in that area. There's that nice big square that you get to walk the outside for the park. But I'd say I'm all over, the Centrum, I'm everywhere. We love Mechanics Hall, we love Foothills Theater, we were at the new opening of the Hanover Theater—love theater. We're patrons of the Worcester County Opera. We're kind of all over the city.

Tracy Cooney
Age 51
Interviewed on November 30, 2006 by Tonia Naughton of Worcester State University

As a young girl growing up near College Hill, I would have picked that as my favorite neighborhood. It was definitely a blue-collar area. It was in the '50s, late '50s, so that everybody's mother was responsible for everybody's kid regardless whether or not they were their own. Every child on the street played together. We did kick the can, we walked to the library together, we read books together outside, we roller-skated together, we did everything as a neighborhood. When I was ten and we moved to the West Side, I didn't find that same close community that I felt on the south side of the city. I don't know if it was because it was a higher socio-economic area.

When I was ten years old, someone tried to get me into a car as I was walking to my friend's house. And I was sent to stay with my cousins for the summer at their farm in the suburbs—actually in the rural area of Massachusetts. And when I came home, my parents told me that they had bought a house on the West Side and that we were moving. So up until that point it was very safe. I don't think it is anymore. [Laughs]

I remember being 16 and getting my license and 290 [highway] had just been extended through south Worcester. And I remember driving there to visit and to travel on 290 was like traveling on Pleasant Street now—it was very limited in the traffic. Now, it's like a speedway, and bumper to bumper, and lots of accidents, and terrifying. Back in the old days, Kelly Square was the only scary place to drive in Worcester. But it seems like everywhere is scary. We spent every Saturday as kids taking the bus downtown. Walking Main Street there were lots of different shops from the 5 and 10 to Denholm's, Filenes, Marcus—lots of high-end stores. And when that left, that was a really disappointing thing. There were terrific movie theaters downtown.

We have so many tremendous neighborhoods of different factions of ethnicity and everything that goes along with it—the culture, the food, the music. I think that's really one of the best things of Worcester.

Cynthia Bizzaro
Age 49
Interviewed on November 2, 2005 by Lauren Wheeler of Worcester State University

We grew up right on the Worcester line. But it mostly changed a lot by development—like almost every place I guess. The Auburn Mall, which is there now, was never there. We lived right behind—and my parents still live there—right behind what's now an industrial park. It used to be a sandpit when we were growing up, and it ended up becoming an industrial park and the other thing that was huge, that I think changed was that 290, the interstate highway, went right through where the industrial park was right behind our house. Our street that we grew up on was a dead end so maybe like six more houses and then at the end of the road is right where the highway went through. There was a pond and I think you can kind of gauge the progress and what happened with the neighborhood a lot by the pond because when my mom grew up here, there was a dance hall and it was an active pond. People would come from all over the town to dance at the dance hall and have parties there, and so it was kind of like a resortish kind of place. And then as the pond got stagnant—and a lot of it I think had to do with the highway going in, with a lot of the development that went around the pond—the dance hall went. We used to fish in it when we were kids, and now there's just nothing worth fishing for in it. So we kind of saw that go downhill. So it changed in that way I think a lot. It's still a community though. I still go, and everybody—the neighbors, their houses are very close together; a lot of the grandkids have taken over the houses.

I think being a small city, I think it gave me a sense—and I still feel that way—of knowing my way around it. I know all the back roads because I grew up here nearby. I think I have a nostalgia for it that comes from a person who's always stayed near home. Since all my life I've lived in or near Worcester, I think I have a nostalgia for how it used to be when I was a kid. Most people do. I can remember instead of taking 290 from Auburn, we travel up Main Street because Main Street goes right into Webster Street right into Auburn. So I can remember the route, and like we'd go and my mom would shop at Denholm's and we'd drop her off. I remember when there was a real downtown. I can still see that. Especially Christmas time, for the holidays when they'd have the displays and stuff and there was Filenes and there was Denholm's. And then I lived with stories of my mother having grown up in the same city, talking about trolleys when they were there. So there was this connectiveness of the city.

I think the two biggest [changes] that I remember would be the Worcester Center, which was the Galleria when they built it, which I think really destroyed Main Street. What happened to Main Street was it was just kind of really hideous. And so there was that structural thing and I think also the highway [290] going through. I didn't, as much as my husband, appreciate the Water Street district. But like the people who lived in the city like Tony did—like on Sundays after church it was the big thing to go up to Water Street, which was where—the Orthodox Temple was there—is still. But the highway went right through that neighborhood, 290 went right through the middle of it.

Kelly Momberger
Age 35
Interviewed on November 2, 2005 by Erin Baron of Worcester State University

I was born in Pittsburgh, Pennsylvania. I see a lot of similarities between Pittsburgh and Worcester. In general, there is the same ethnic mix. There is an industrial area but also lots of arts organizations and creativity as well as universities.

Worcester has had a pretty significant impact on me. I really like that Worcester is sort of the small-town big-city. I keep running into people in one place that I know from some other completely unrelated place. You form these great networks and the more your network expands, the more you find out about new and interesting things to do.

A woman who is a friend of my landlord is actually a very good friend with the woman I knit with. The man that I run the theatre company [Red Feather Theatre Company] with, told me that he wants a professor from Worcester State College to write a play about an event that took place 250 years ago. I said, "The woman who knows my landlord, who is a friend of the woman I knit with, did a whole exhibit on the very thing and they should get together." It's just amazing how these things happen, but it's great.

Worcester is the kind of community where you actually make an impact. You can start something up and see it happen. Worcester attracts all kinds of people. We have artists, writers, and a large number of immigrants. We have vibrancy and multi-culturalism.

Some people who live here may say that there is nothing to do. But how can they say that? I could be busy every night of the week. Some people need to open themselves up and not buy into the negative stereotype. Most people in Worcester really love it here. Some people who come here for schools or jobs start bellyaching. We throw events all the time and it's like pulling teeth to get some people to leave their homes. And it's frustrating because at the same time they are the ones who are complaining that there's nothing to do. Do they want me to go to their houses and pick them up?

Worcester has a lot of smart people and I think that sometimes this is overlooked. We have so many people employed by the biotech industry and by the universities.

Interesting things are happening here every day, and you don't really hear about it. I love the diversity in Worcester and the architecture. I know people badmouth the triple-deckers, but I think they're great. There is so much that is unique here, a unique mix of everything. We have immigrants and people who have lived here their whole lives. And it all kind of ties together. There's always something new and different that you can learn about that's going on right under your nose.

I think that right now is a really good time for women in Worcester because we live in a place with so many interesting opportunities. They've legalized gay marriage, tattoos, and liquor on Sundays, so there's really no reason to leave now!

BIBLIOGRAPHY

Bowden, Edwin T. (Ed.). *The Satiric Poems of John Trumbull: The Progress of Dulness (sic) and M'Fingal.* Austin, TX: University of Texas, 1962.

Clarke, Edward H. *Sex in Education; or, A Fair Chance for Girls.* Boston: Houghton, Mifflin & Company, 1873.

Collins, Gail. *America's Women: 400 Years of Dolls, Drudges, Helpmates, and Heroines.* New York: HarperCollins Publishers, 2003.

Conway, Jill. "Women's Place." *Change* 10 (1978, March): 8-9.

Cross, Patricia K. "The Woman Student." *Women in Higher Education.* Eds. W. Todd Furniss and Patricia Albjerg Graham. Washington, D.C.: American Council on Education, 1972. 29-50.

Cunningham, Patricia. A. *Reforming Women's Fashion, 1850-1920: Politics, Health, and Art.* Ohio: Kent State University Press, 2003.

Gilman, Charlotte Perkins. "The Yellow Wallpaper." *The New England Magazine,* 11.5. (1892, January): 647-56.

Mass, Wendy. *Women's Rights,* Lucent Books, Inc., 1998.

Matthews, Glenna. *The Rise of Public Woman: Woman's Power and Woman's Place in the United States, 1630-1970.* New York: Oxford University Press, 1992.

McClymer, John. F. *This High and Holy Moment: The First National Woman's Rights Convention, Worcester, 1850.* Ft. Worth: Harcourt Brace College Publishers, 1999.

McCutcheon, Marc. *Everyday Life in the 1880s, a Guide for Writers, Students & Historians.* Writer's Digest Books, 1993.

McMillen, Sally A. *Seneca Falls and the Origins of the Women's Rights Movement.* New York: Oxford University Press, 2008.

More, Ellen S. *Restoring the Balance: Women Physicians and the Profession of Medicine, 1850-1995.* Cambridge, MA: Harvard University Press, 1999.

"Newspaper Accounts of the 1850 Convention." *Proceedings, 1850 Woman's Rights Convention, Assumption College.* 6 June 2010. <http://www.1.assumption.edu/WHW/old/newspaper%20accounts_1850.html>

O'Toole, John M. *Tornado! 84 Minutes, 94 Lives.* Worcester, MA: Chandler House Press, 1993.

"Proceedings of the 1850 National Woman's Rights Convention of 1850." *Historical Library, Worcester Women's History Project.* 6 June 2010. <http://www.wwhp.org.>

Solomon, Barbara Miller. *In the Company of Educated Women.* New Haven: Yale University Press, 1985.

U.S. Census Bureau. *Educational Attainment in the United States 2010.* <http://www.census.gov>

Weatherford, Doris. *American Women's History, An A to Z of People, Organizations, Issues, and Events.* New York: Prentice Hall, Inc., 1994.

"Why Worcester?" *Historical Library, Worcester Women's History Project.* 6 June 2010. <http://www.wwhp.org.>

"Women's History in America." *Women's International Center.* 18 August 2011. <http://www.wic.org/misc/history.htm>

Worcester Women's History Project. *Worcester Women's History Heritage Trail: Worcester in the Struggle for Equality in the Mid-Nineteenth Century.* Worcester, MA: WWHP, 2002.

INDEX

Akpan, Mercy, 79
Aleksiewicz, Mary, 96
Anderson, Mary Lou, 147
Aschkenase, Thea, 155
Bassett, Kay, 74
Bizzaro, Cynthia, 182
Caruso, Nancy, 50
Chandler, Harriette, 135
Coleman, Shirley, 173
Connolly, Donna, 44
Connolly, Lori, 114
Constantin, Clair, 53
Cooney, Tracy, 180
Courtemanche, Dolores, 165
Cummings, Mildred, 64
Dean, Elizabeth, 152
Dearborn, Margery, 164
Demarais, Melanie, 143
Donnelly, Carol, 174
Donovan, Patricia, 117
Dore, Charlyne, 177
Elissondo, Guillermina, 54
England, Gail, 84
Gautier, Aida, 41
Gordon, Brenda, 51
Hakim, Nora Antoun, 17
Haller, Barbara, 141
Hein, Hilde, 31
Hill, Jean Laquidera, 87
Hoskins, Betty, 35
Howie, Laura, 34
Jepson, Judith, 172
Johnson, Carrie, 76
Kelly, Lee Norton, 145
Klump, Ann, 116

Laipson, Hannah, 20
Levine, Frances, 162
Lewandowski, Suzanne, 121
Lucier, Genevieve, 62
Marshall, Rosemary, 80
Masiello, Pat, 110
McCarron, Ann, 127
McKenna, Mary Jane, 139
McLaughlin, Maureen, 66
McNeil, Ogretta, 28
Milkowski, Anne, 106
Miller, Linda Antoun, 39
Momberger, Kelly, 183
Murphy, Barbara, 168
Nigrosh, Gale, 71
O'Connor, Kathleen, 69
O'Neill, Theresa, 167
Pandolfi, Tara, 103
Pellegrino, Ivana, 82
Penny, Angela, 178
Phillips, Alexandria, 119
Quintal, Claire, 25
Robertson, Sara, 137
Ross, Dorian, 24
Safford, Brenda, 47
Sanchez, Wilma, 123
Schwartz, Zelda, 170
Skehan, Carol, 67
Swain, Virginia, 150
Vayo, Samantha, 105
White, Judith, 104
Wilcox, Joanne, 98
Williams, Jill, 90
Young, Lynda, 100

ABOUT THE AUTHORS

Maureen Ryan Doyle has worked as a freelance writer for many years and is also the owner of a small property management company in Central Massachusetts. She was the winner of *Good Housekeeping Magazine's* New Traditionalist writing competition. Maureen earned her B.A. degree in History from Assumption College where she was a member of the first undergraduate class of women. She has pursued graduate study at Emerson College in Boston and Oglethorpe University in Atlanta. She and her husband, Francis X. Doyle, reside in Holden, Massachusetts. Their family includes their daughter, Maryssa, and son and daughter-in-law Colin and Dani Doyle.

Charlene L. Martin, Ed.D. has over thirty years of experience in higher education. She is the former Dean of Continuing Education at Assumption College and the founding director of the Worcester Institute for Senior Education known as WISE. She earned her B.A. and M.A. from Assumption College and her Doctorate in Educational Policy, Research, and Administration with a specialty in Higher Education from the University of Massachusetts Amherst. She is an adjunct professor and her research and publications focus on educational opportunities for older adults in retirement. She and her husband, Jim Martin, live in Shrewsbury, Massachusetts.

Both Maureen and Charlene serve on the Steering Committee of the Worcester Women's History Project and have co-chaired the Worcester Women's Oral History Project since 2008.

We hope that you have enjoyed reading about some fascinating women of the greater Worcester area. These excerpts are taken from edited transcripts many of which can be found in their entirety on the WWHP website.

The work of the Worcester Women's Oral History Project is ongoing with new interviews currently being scheduled. Would you like to be interviewed? Do you know someone who would like to be interviewed? If so, please contact us at www.wwhp.org, click on Oral History Project, and then click on Share Your Story.

Made in the USA
Charleston, SC
12 December 2011